SIMULINK®
STUDENT VERSION

Learning SIMULINK
Version 3.0 (Release 11)

How to Contact The MathWorks:

```
www.mathworks.com          Web
ftp.mathworks.com          Anonymous FTP server
comp.soft-sys.matlab       Newsgroup
```

```
support@mathworks.com      Technical support
suggest@mathworks.com      Product enhancement suggestions
bugs@mathworks.com         Bug reports
doc@mathworks.com          Documentation error reports
subscribe@mathworks.com    Subscribing user registration
service@mathworks.com      Order status, license renewals, passcodes
info@mathworks.com         Sales, pricing, and general information
```

508-647-7000   Phone

508-647-7001   Fax

The MathWorks, Inc.   Mail
3 Apple Hill Drive
Natick, MA 01760-2098

ISBN 0-9672195-2-3

Learning Simulink

© COPYRIGHT 1999 by The MathWorks, Inc.

The software described in this document is furnished under a license agreement. The software may be used or copied only under the terms of the license agreement. No part of this manual may be photocopied or reproduced in any form without prior written consent from The MathWorks, Inc.

FEDERAL ACQUISITION: This provision applies to all acquisitions of the Program and Documentation by or for the federal government of the United States. By accepting delivery of the Program, the government hereby agrees that this software qualifies as "commercial" computer software within the meaning of FAR Part 12.212, DFARS Part 227.7202-1, DFARS Part 227.7202-3, DFARS Part 252.227-7013, and DFARS Part 252.227-7014. The terms and conditions of The MathWorks, Inc. Software License Agreement shall pertain to the government's use and disclosure of the Program and Documentation, and shall supersede any conflicting contractual terms or conditions. If this license fails to meet the government's minimum needs or is inconsistent in any respect with federal procurement law, the government agrees to return the Program and Documentation, unused, to MathWorks.

MATLAB, Simulink, Stateflow, Handle Graphics, and Real-Time Workshop are registered trademarks, and Target Language Compiler is a trademark of The MathWorks, Inc.

Other product or brand names are trademarks or registered trademarks of their respective holders.

Printing History: August 1999   First printing   New manual

Contents

Introduction
1

About the Student Version 1-2
   Student Use Policy 1-2
   Differences Between the Student Version
   and the Professional Version 1-3

Obtaining Additional MathWorks Products 1-5
   Patches and Updates 1-5

Getting Started with Simulink 1-6

Finding Reference Information 1-7

Troubleshooting and Other Resources 1-8
   Documentation Library 1-8
      Accessing the Online Documentation 1-8
   Usenet Newsgroup 1-9
   MathWorks Web Site 1-9
   MathWorks Education Web Site 1-9
   MATLAB Related Books 1-9
   MathWorks Store 1-9
   MathWorks Knowledge Base 1-10
   Technical Support 1-10
      Student Version Support Policy 1-10
   Product Registration 1-10

About Simulink 1-11
   What Is Simulink? 1-11
   How to Use This Manual 1-12

i

2 Quick Start

Running a Demo Model 2-2
    Description of the Demo 2-3
    Some Things to Try 2-4
    What This Demo Illustrates 2-5
    Other Useful Demos 2-5

Building a Simple Model 2-6

3 Creating a Model

Starting Simulink 3-2
    Creating a New Model 3-3
    Editing an Existing Model 3-3
    Entering Simulink Commands 3-3
        Using the Simulink Menu Bar to Enter Commands 3-3
        Using Context-Sensitive Menus to Enter Commands ... 3-4
        Using the Simulink Toolbar to Enter Commands 3-4
        Using the MATLAB Window to Enter Commands 3-4
        Undoing a Command 3-5
    Simulink Windows 3-5
        Status Bar 3-5
    Zooming Block Diagrams 3-6

Selecting Objects 3-7
    Selecting One Object 3-7
    Selecting More than One Object 3-7
        Selecting Multiple Objects One at a Time 3-7
        Selecting Multiple Objects Using a Bounding Box 3-7
        Selecting the Entire Model 3-8

Blocks 3-9
    Block Data Tips 3-9
    Virtual Blocks 3-9

Copying and Moving Blocks from One Window to Another .. **3-10**
Moving Blocks in a Model **3-12**
Duplicating Blocks in a Model **3-12**
Specifying Block Parameters **3-12**
Block Properties Dialog Box **3-13**
   Description **3-13**
   Priority **3-14**
   Tag **3-14**
   Open Function **3-14**
   Attributes Format String **3-14**
Deleting Blocks **3-14**
Changing the Orientation of Blocks **3-15**
Resizing Blocks **3-15**
Manipulating Block Names **3-16**
   Changing Block Names **3-16**
   Changing the Location of a Block Name **3-17**
   Changing Whether a Block Name Appears **3-17**
Displaying Parameters Beneath a Block's Icon **3-17**
Disconnecting Blocks **3-18**
Vector Input and Output **3-18**
Scalar Expansion of Inputs and Parameters **3-18**
   Scalar Expansion of Inputs **3-18**
   Scalar Expansion of Parameters **3-19**
Assigning Block Priorities **3-19**
Using Drop Shadows **3-20**

Libraries **3-21**
Terminology **3-21**
Copying a Library Block into a Model **3-21**
Updating a Linked Block **3-23**
Breaking a Link to a Library Block **3-23**
Finding the Library Block for a Reference Block **3-24**
Getting Information About Library Blocks **3-24**

Browsing Block Libraries 3-24
    Navigating the Library Tree 3-25
    Searching Libraries 3-25
    Opening a Library 3-25
    Creating and Opening Models 3-25
    Copying Blocks 3-25
    Displaying Help on a Block 3-25
    Pinning the Library Browser 3-26

Lines 3-27
    Drawing a Line Between Blocks 3-27
    Drawing a Branch Line 3-28
    Drawing a Line Segment 3-28
    Moving a Line Segment 3-29
    Dividing a Line into Segments 3-29
    Moving a Line Vertex 3-30
    Displaying Line Widths 3-31
    Inserting Blocks in a Line 3-31
    Signal Labels 3-32
    Using Signal Labels 3-33

Annotations 3-34

Summary of Mouse and Keyboard Actions 3-35

Creating Subsystems 3-38
    Creating a Subsystem by Adding the Subsystem Block 3-38
    Creating a Subsystem by Grouping Existing Blocks 3-39
    Labeling Subsystem Ports 3-40
    Using Callback Routines 3-40

Tips for Building Models 3-44

Modeling Equations 3-45
    Converting Celsius to Fahrenheit 3-45
    Modeling a Simple Continuous System 3-46

Saving a Model 3-48

Printing a Block Diagram 3-49
   Print Dialog Box 3-49
   Print Command 3-50
   Specifying Paper Size and Orientation 3-51
   Positioning and Sizing a Diagram 3-51

The Model Browser 3-53
   Using the Model Browser on Windows 3-53
   Using the Model Browser on Linux 3-54
      Contents of the Browser Window 3-54
      Interpreting List Contents 3-55
      Opening a System 3-55
      Looking into a Masked System or a Linked Block 3-56
      Displaying List Contents Alphabetically 3-56

Ending a Simulink Session 3-57

4

Running a Simulation

Introduction 4-2
   Using Menu Commands 4-2
   Running a Simulation from the Command Line 4-3

Running a Simulation Using Menu Commands 4-4
   Setting Simulation Parameters and Choosing the Solver 4-4
   Applying the Simulation Parameters 4-4
   Starting the Simulation 4-4
   Simulation Diagnostics Dialog Box 4-6

v

The Simulation Parameters Dialog Box 4-8
   The Solver Page 4-8
      Simulation Time 4-9
      Solvers 4-9
      Solver Options 4-12
      Step Sizes 4-12
      Error Tolerances 4-13
      The Maximum Order for ode15s 4-14
      Multitasking Options 4-15
      Output Options 4-15
   The Workspace I/O Page 4-17
      Loading Input from the Base Workspace 4-17
      Saving Output to the Workspace 4-20
      Loading and Saving States 4-21
   The Diagnostics Page 4-24
      Consistency Checking 4-24
      Disabling Zero Crossing Detection 4-25
      Disable Optimized I/O Storage 4-25
      Relax Boolean Type Checking (2.x Compatible) 4-26

Improving Simulation Performance and Accuracy 4-27
   Speeding Up the Simulation 4-27
   Improving Simulation Accuracy 4-28

5

Analyzing Simulation Results

Viewing Output Trajectories 5-2
   Using the Scope Block 5-2
   Using Return Variables 5-2
   Using the To Workspace Block 5-3

Linearization 5-4

Equilibrium Point Determination 5-7

6 Using Masks to Customize Blocks

Introduction 6-2

A Sample Masked Subsystem 6-3
    Creating Mask Dialog Box Prompts 6-4
    Creating the Block Description and Help Text 6-6
    Creating the Block Icon 6-6
    Summary 6-8

The Mask Editor: An Overview 6-9

The Initialization Page 6-10
    Prompts and Associated Variables 6-10
        Creating the First Prompt 6-11
        Inserting a Prompt 6-11
        Editing a Prompt 6-11
        Deleting a Prompt 6-12
        Moving a Prompt 6-12
    Control Types 6-12
        Defining an Edit Control 6-12
        Defining a Check Box Control 6-13
        Defining a Pop-Up Control 6-13
    Default Values for Masked Block Parameters 6-14
    Tunable Parameters 6-14
    Initialization Commands 6-15
        The Mask Workspace 6-15
        Debugging Initialization Commands 6-17

The Icon Page 6-18
    Displaying Text on the Block Icon 6-18
    Displaying Graphics on the Block Icon 6-20

Displaying Images on Masks 6-21
Displaying a Transfer Function on the Block Icon 6-22
Controlling Icon Properties 6-23
   Icon Frame 6-23
   Icon Transparency 6-24
   Icon Rotation 6-24
   Drawing Coordinates 6-24

The Documentation Page 6-26
   The Mask Type Field 6-26
   The Block Description Field 6-26
   The Mask Help Text Field 6-27

7 Additional Topics

How Simulink Works 7-2
   Zero Crossings 7-3
      State Event Handling 7-3
      Integration of Discontinuous Signals 7-3
      Implementation Details 7-4
      Caveat 7-5
      Blocks with Zero Crossings 7-6
   Algebraic Loops 7-7
      Nonalgebraic Direct-Feedthrough Loops 7-9
   Invariant Constants 7-11

Discrete-Time Systems 7-13
   Discrete Blocks 7-13
   Sample Time 7-13
   Purely Discrete Systems 7-13
   Multirate Systems 7-14
   Sample Time Colors 7-15
   Mixed Continuous and Discrete Systems 7-17

8

Simulink Debugger

Introduction 8-2

Using the Debugger 8-3
   Starting the Debugger 8-3
   Getting Help 8-4
   Entering Commands 8-4
   About Block Indexes 8-4
   Accessing the MATLAB Workspace 8-4

Running a Simulation Incrementally 8-6
   Stepping by Blocks 8-6
      Crossing a Time Step Boundary 8-7
      Stepping by Minor Time Steps 8-7
   Stepping by Time Steps 8-7
   Stepping by Breakpoints 8-8
   Running a Simulation Nonstop 8-8

Setting Breakpoints 8-9
   Breaking at Blocks 8-9
      Breaking at a Block's Beginning 8-10
      Breaking at a Block's End 8-11
      Clearing Breakpoints from Blocks 8-11
   Breaking at Time Steps 8-11
   Breaking on Nonfinite Values 8-11
   Breaking on Step-Size Limiting Steps 8-12
   Breaking at Zero-Crossings 8-12

Displaying Information About the Simulation 8-13
   Displaying Block I/O 8-13
      probe Command 8-13
      disp Command 8-14
      trace Command 8-14
   Displaying Algebraic Loop Information 8-14
   Displaying System States 8-15
   Displaying Integration Information 8-15

Displaying Information About the Model **8-17**
    Displaying a Model's Block Execution Order 8-17
    Displaying a Block 8-17
    Displaying a Model's Nonvirtual Systems 8-18
    Displaying a Model's Nonvirtual Blocks 8-18
    Displaying Blocks with Potential Zero-Crossings 8-19
    Displaying Algebraic Loops 8-20
    Displaying Debug Settings 8-20

Debugger Command Reference **8-21**

Simulink Quick Reference

A

Introduction

About the Student Version	1-2
Obtaining Additional MathWorks Products	1-5
Getting Started with Simulink	1-6
Finding Reference Information	1-7
Troubleshooting and Other Resources	1-8
About Simulink	1-11

1 Introduction

About the Student Version

The Student Version of MATLAB® & Simulink® is the premier software package for technical computation, data analysis, and visualization in education and industry. The Student Version of MATLAB & Simulink provides all of the features of professional MATLAB, with no limitations, and the full functionality of professional Simulink, with model sizes up to 300 blocks. The Student Version gives you immediate access to the high-performance numeric computing power you need.

MATLAB allows you to focus on your course work and applications rather than on programming details. It enables you to solve many numerical problems in a fraction of the time it would take you to write a program in a lower level language. MATLAB helps you better understand and apply concepts in applications ranging from engineering and mathematics to chemistry, biology, and economics.

Simulink, included with the Student Version, provides a block diagram tool for modeling and simulating dynamical systems, including signal processing, controls, communications, and other complex systems.

The Symbolic Math Toolbox, also included with the Student Version, is based on the Maple® V symbolic kernel and lets you perform symbolic computations and variable-precision arithmetic.

MATLAB products are used in a broad range of industries, including automotive, aerospace, electronics, environmental, telecommunications, computer peripherals, finance, and medical. More than 400,000 technical professionals at the world's most innovative technology companies, government research labs, financial institutions, and at more than 2,000 universities rely on MATLAB and Simulink as the fundamental tools for their engineering and scientific work.

Student Use Policy

This Student License is for use in conjunction with courses offered at a degree-granting institution. The MathWorks offers this license as a special service to the student community and asks your help in seeing that its terms are not abused.

To use this Student License, you must be a student using the software in conjunction with courses offered at degree-granting institutions.

You may not use this Student License at a company or government lab, or if you are an instructor at a university. Also, you may not use it for research or for commercial or industrial purposes. In these cases, you can acquire the appropriate professional or academic version of the software by contacting The MathWorks.

Differences Between the Student Version and the Professional Version

MATLAB

This version of MATLAB provides full support for all language features as well as graphics, external (Application Program Interface) support, and access to every other feature of the professional version of MATLAB.

Note MATLAB does not have a matrix size limitation in this Student Version.

MATLAB Differences. There are a few small differences between the Student Version and the professional version of MATLAB:

1 The MATLAB prompt in the Student Version is

   `EDU>>`

2 The window title bars include the words

   `<Student Version>`

3 All printouts contain the footer

   `Student Version of MATLAB`

   This footer is not an option that can be turned off; it will always appear in your printouts.

Simulink

This Student Version contains the complete Simulink product, which is used with MATLAB to model, simulate, and analyze dynamical systems.

Simulink Differences.

1 Models are limited to 300 blocks.

2 The window title bars include the words

    <Student Version>

3 All printouts contain the footer

    Student Version of MATLAB

   This footer is not an option that can be turned off; it will always appear in your printouts.

Obtaining Additional MathWorks Products

Many college courses recommend MATLAB as their standard instructional software. In some cases, the courses may require particular toolboxes, blocksets, or other products. Many of these products are available for student use. You may purchase and download these additional products at special student prices from the MathWorks Store at www.mathworks.com/store.

Although many professional toolboxes are available at student prices from the MathWorks Store, *not* every one is available for student use. Some of the toolboxes you can purchase include:

Communications	Neural Network
Control System	Optimization
Fuzzy Logic	Signal Processing
Image Processing	Statistics

For an up-to-date list of which toolboxes are available, visit the MathWorks Store.

Note The toolboxes that are available for the Student Version of MATLAB & Simulink have the same functionality as the full, professional versions. However, these student versions will *only* work with the Student Version. Likewise, the professional versions of the toolboxes will *not* work with the Student Version.

Patches and Updates

From time to time, the MathWorks makes changes to some of its products between scheduled releases. When this happens, these updates are made available from our Web site. As a registered user of the Student Version, you will be notified by e-mail of the availability of product updates.

Note To register your product, see "Product Registration" in "Troubleshooting and Other Resources" in this chapter.

Getting Started with Simulink

What I Want	What I Should Do
I need to install Simulink.	See Chapter 2, "Installation," in the *Learning MATLAB* book.
I'm new to Simulink and want to learn it quickly.	Start by reading *Learning Simulink*. You'll learn how to model, simulate, and analyze dynamical systems. Since Simulink is graphical and interactive, this book encourages you to use it quickly. You can access the rest of the Simulink documentation from the online help (Help Desk).
I want to look at some samples of what you can do with Simulink.	There are numerous demonstrations included with Simulink. You can see the demos by selecting **Examples and Demos** from the **Help** menu. (Linux users type demo at the MATLAB prompt.) There are Simulink demos for simple models, complex models, and advanced products. You also will find a large selection of demos at www.mathworks.com/demos.

Finding Reference Information

What I Want	What I Should Do
I want to know how to use a specific Simulink block.	Use the online help (Help Desk) facility by using the command `helpdesk`, or by selecting **Help Desk** from the **Help** menu on the PC. The Simulink blocks are described in *Using Simulink*.
I want to find a block for a specific purpose but I don't know its name.	There are several choices: • See Appendix A, "Simulink Quick Reference," in this book for a list of Simulink blocks. • From the Help Desk peruse the Block Reference section in *Using Simulink*. • Use the full text search from the Help Desk.
I want to know what blocks are available in a general area.	Use the Help Desk to see the Block Reference section in *Using Simulink*, or see Appendix A, "Simulink Quick Reference," in this book for a list of Simulink blocks.

Troubleshooting and Other Resources

What I Want	What I Should Do
I have a Simulink specific problem I want help with.	Visit the Technical Support section (www.mathworks.com/support) of the MathWorks Web site and use the Solution Support Engine to search the Knowledge Base of problem solutions.
I want to report a bug or make a suggestion.	Use the Help Desk or send e-mail to bugs@mathworks.com or suggest@mathworks.com.

Documentation Library

Your Student Version of MATLAB & Simulink contains much more documentation than the two printed books, *Learning MATLAB* and *Learning Simulink*. On your CD is a personal reference library of every book and reference page distributed by The MathWorks. Access this documentation library from the Help Desk.

Note Even though you have the documentation set for the MathWorks family of products, not every product is available for the Student Version of MATLAB & Simulink. For an up-to-date list of available products, visit the MathWorks Store. At the store you can also purchase printed manuals for the MATLAB family of products.

Accessing the Online Documentation

Access the online documentation (Help Desk) directly from your product CD. (Linux users should refer to Chapter 2, "Installation," in the *Learning MATLAB* book for specific information on configuring and accessing the Help Desk from the CD.)

1 Place the CD in your CD-ROM drive.

2 Select **Documentation (Help Desk)** from the **Help** menu.

The Help Desk appears in a Web browser.

Usenet Newsgroup

If you have access to Usenet newsgroups, you can join the active community of participants in the MATLAB specific group, comp.soft-sys.matlab. This forum is a gathering of professionals and students who use MATLAB and have questions or comments about it and its associated products. This is a great resource for posing questions and answering those of others. MathWorks staff also participates actively in this newsgroup.

MathWorks Web Site

Use your browser to visit the MathWorks Web site, www.mathworks.com. You'll find lots of information about MathWorks products and how they are used in education and industry, product demos, and MATLAB based books. From the Web site you will also be able to access our technical support resources, view a library of user and company supplied M-files, and get information about products and upcoming events.

MathWorks Education Web Site

This education-specific Web site, www.mathworks.com/education, contains many resources for various branches of mathematics and science. Many of these include teaching examples, books, and other related products. You will also find a comprehensive list of links to Web sites where MATLAB is used for teaching and research at universities.

MATLAB Related Books

Hundreds of MATLAB related books are available from many different publishers. An up-to-date list is available at www.mathworks.com/books.

MathWorks Store

The MathWorks Store (www.mathworks.com/store) gives you an easy way to purchase products, upgrades, and documentation.

Introduction

MathWorks Knowledge Base

You can access the MathWorks Knowledge Base from the Support link on our Web site. Our Technical Support group maintains this database of frequently asked questions (FAQ). You can peruse the Knowledge Base by topics, categories, or use the Solution Search Engine to quickly locate relevant data. You can answer many of your questions by spending a few minutes with this around-the-clock resource.

Also, Technical Notes, which is accessible from our Technical Support Web site (www.mathworks.com/support), contains numerous examples on graphics, mathematics, API, Simulink, and others.

Technical Support

Registered users of the Student Version of MATLAB & Simulink can use our electronic technical support services to answer product questions. Visit our Technical Support Web site at www.mathworks.com/support.

Student Version Support Policy

The MathWorks does not provide telephone technical support to users of the Student Version of MATLAB & Simulink. There are numerous other vehicles of technical support that you can use. The Sources of Information card included with the Student Version identifies the ways to obtain support.

After checking the available MathWorks sources for help, if you still cannot resolve your problem, you should contact your instructor. Your instructor should be able to help you, but if not, there is telephone technical support for registered instructors who have adopted the Student Version of MATLAB & Simulink in their courses.

Product Registration

Visit the MathWorks Web site (www.mathworks.com/student) and register your Student Version.

About Simulink

Welcome to Simulink! In the last few years, Simulink has become the most widely used software package in academia and industry for modeling and simulating dynamical systems.

Simulink encourages you to try things out. You can easily build models from scratch, or take an existing model and add to it. Simulations are interactive, so you can change parameters "on the fly" and immediately see what happens. You have instant access to all of the analysis tools in MATLAB, so you can take the results and analyze and visualize them. We hope that you will get a sense of the *fun* of modeling and simulation, through an environment that encourages you to pose a question, model it, and see what happens.

With Simulink, you can move beyond idealized linear models to explore more realistic nonlinear models, factoring in friction, air resistance, gear slippage, hard stops, and the other things that describe real-world phenomena. It turns your computer into a lab for modeling and analyzing systems that simply wouldn't be possible or practical otherwise, whether the behavior of an automotive clutch system, the flutter of an airplane wing, the dynamics of a predator-prey model, or the effect of the monetary supply on the economy.

Simulink is also practical. With thousands of engineers around the world using it to model and solve real problems, knowledge of this tool will serve you well throughout your professional career.

We hope you enjoy exploring the software.

What Is Simulink?

Simulink is a software package for modeling, simulating, and analyzing dynamical systems. It supports linear and nonlinear systems, modeled in continuous time, sampled time, or a hybrid of the two. Systems can also be multirate, i.e., have different parts that are sampled or updated at different rates.

For modeling, Simulink provides a graphical user interface (GUI) for building models as block diagrams, using click-and-drag mouse operations. With this interface, you can draw the models just as you would with pencil and paper (or as most textbooks depict them). This is a far cry from previous simulation packages that require you to formulate differential equations and difference equations in a language or program. Simulink includes a comprehensive block library of sinks, sources, linear and nonlinear components, and connectors. You can also customize and create your own blocks. For information on creating your own blocks, see the separate *Writing S-Functions* guide.

Models are hierarchical, so you can build models using both top-down and bottom-up approaches. You can view the system at a high level, then double-click on blocks to go down through the levels to see increasing levels of model detail. This approach provides insight into how a model is organized and how its parts interact.

After you define a model, you can simulate it, using a choice of integration methods, either from the Simulink menus or by entering commands in MATLAB's command window. The menus are particularly convenient for interactive work, while the command-line approach is very useful for running a batch of simulations (for example, if you are doing Monte Carlo simulations or want to sweep a parameter across a range of values). Using scopes and other display blocks, you can see the simulation results while the simulation is running. In addition, you can change parameters and immediately see what happens, for "what if" exploration. The simulation results can be put in the MATLAB workspace for postprocessing and visualization.

Model analysis tools include linearization and trimming tools, which can be accessed from the MATLAB command line, plus the many tools in MATLAB and its application toolboxes. And because MATLAB and Simulink are integrated, you can simulate, analyze, and revise your models in either environment at any point.

How to Use This Manual

Because Simulink is graphical and interactive, we encourage you to jump right in and try it.

For a useful introduction that will help you start using Simulink quickly, take a look at "Running a Demo Model" in Chapter 2. Browse around the model, double-click on blocks that look interesting, and you will quickly get a sense of how Simulink works. If you want a quick lesson in building a model, see "Building a Simple Model" in Chapter 2.

Chapter 3 describes in detail how to build and edit a model. It also discusses how to save and print a model and provides some useful tips.

Chapter 4 describes how Simulink performs a simulation. It covers simulation parameters and the integration solvers used for simulation, including some of the strengths and weaknesses of each solver that should help you choose the appropriate solver for your problem. It also discusses multirate and hybrid systems.

Chapter 5 discusses Simulink and MATLAB features useful for viewing and analyzing simulation results.

Chapter 6 discusses methods for creating your own blocks and using masks to customize their appearance and use.

Chapter 7 provides information about how Simulink works, including information about zero crossings, algebraic loops, and discrete and hybrid systems.

Chapter 8 explains how to use the Simulink debugger to debug Simulink models.

Appendix A provides a quick reference for the Simulink blocks.

Although we have tried to provide the most complete and up-to-date information in this manual, some information may have changed after it was completed. Please check the online *Known Software and Documentation Problems* accessible from the Help Desk, for the latest release notes.

1 Introduction

Quick Start

Running a Demo Model 2-2
Description of the Demo 2-3
Some Things to Try 2-4
What This Demo Illustrates 2-5
Other Useful Demos 2-5

Building a Simple Model 2-6

2 Quick Start

Running a Demo Model

An interesting demo program provided with Simulink models the thermodynamics of a house. To run this demo, follow these steps:

1 Start MATLAB. See your MATLAB documentation if you're not sure how to do this.

2 Run the demo model by typing `thermo` in the MATLAB command window. This command starts up Simulink and creates a model window that contains this model.

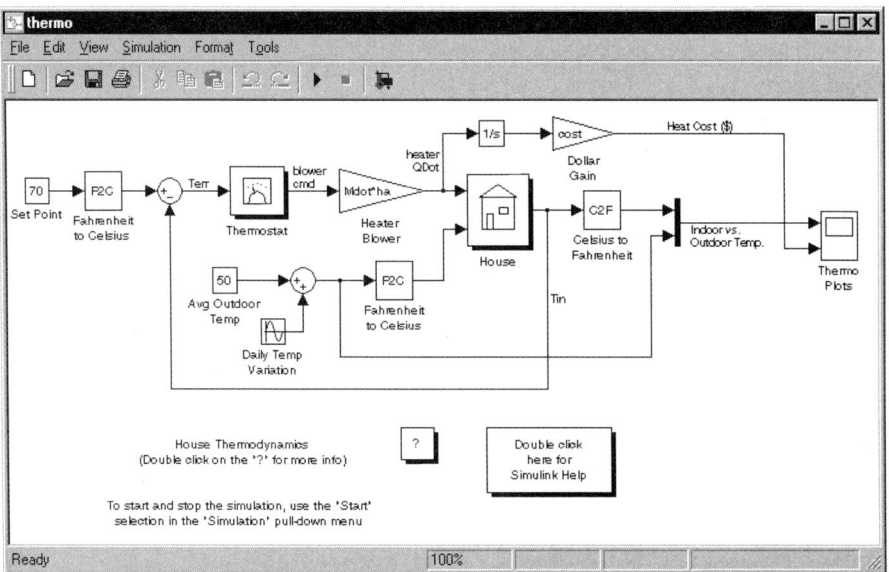

When you open the model, Simulink opens a Scope block containing two plots labeled Indoor vs. Outdoor Temp and Heat Cost ($), respectively.

3 To start the simulation, pull down the **Simulation** menu and choose the **Start** command (or, on Microsoft Windows, press the **Start** button on the Simulink toolbar). As the simulation runs, the indoor and outdoor temperatures appear in the Indoor vs. Outdoor Temp plot and the cumulative heating cost appears in the Heat Cost ($) plot.

Running a Demo Model

4 To stop the simulation, choose the **Stop** command from the **Simulation** menu (or press the **Pause** button on the toolbar). If you want to explore other parts of the model, look over the suggestions in "Some Things to Try" on page 2-4.

5 When you're finished running the simulation, close the model by choosing **Close** from the **File** menu.

Description of the Demo

The demo models the thermodynamics of a house using a simple model. The thermostat is set to 70 degrees Fahrenheit and is affected by the outside temperature, which varies by applying a sine wave with amplitude of 15 degrees to a base temperature of 50 degrees. This simulates daily temperature fluctuations.

The model uses subsystems to simplify the model diagram and create reusable systems. A subsystem is a group of blocks that is represented by a Subsystem block. This model contains five subsystems: one named Thermostat, one named House, and three Temp Convert subsystems (two convert Fahrenheit to Celsius, one converts Celsius to Fahrenheit).

The internal and external temperatures are fed into the House subsystem, which updates the internal temperature. Double-click on the House block to see the underlying blocks in that subsystem.

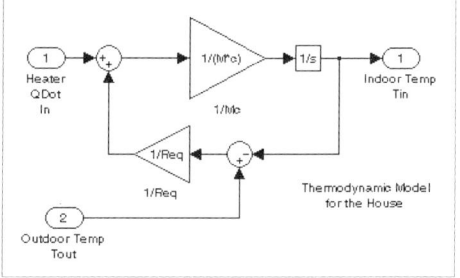

House subsystem

The Thermostat subsystem models the operation of a thermostat, determining when the heating system is turned on and off. Double-click on the block to see the underlying blocks in that subsystem.

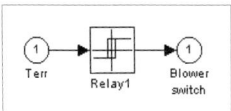 Thermostat subsystem

Both the outside and inside temperatures are converted from Fahrenheit to Celsius by identical subsystems

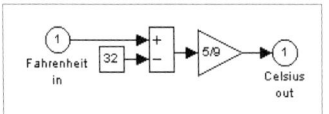 Fahrenheit to Celsius conversion (F2C)

When the heat is on, the heating costs are computed and displayed on the Heat Cost ($) plot on the Thermo Plots Scope. The internal temperature is displayed on the Indoor Temp Scope.

Some Things to Try

Here are several things to try to see how the model responds to different parameters:

- Each Scope block contains one or more signal display areas and controls that enable you to select the range of the signal displayed, zoom in on a portion of the signal, and perform other useful tasks. The horizontal axis represents time and the vertical axis represents the signal value. For more information about the Scope block, see the Scope block in the online reference pages.
- The Constant block labeled Set Point (at the top left of the model) sets the desired internal temperature. Open this block and reset the value to 80 degrees while the simulation is running. See how the indoor temperature and heating costs change. Also, adjust the outside temperature (the Avg Outdoor Temp block) and see how it affects the simulation.
- Adjust the daily temperature variation by opening the Sine Wave block labeled Daily Temp Variation and changing the **Amplitude** parameter.

What This Demo Illustrates

This demo illustrates several tasks commonly used when building models:

- Running the simulation involves specifying parameters and starting the simulation with the **Start** command, described in detail in Chapter 4.
- You can encapsulate complex groups of related blocks in a single block, called a subsystem. Creating subsystems is described in detail in Chapter 3.
- You can create a customized icon and design a dialog box for a block by using the masking feature, described in detail in Chapter 6. In the thermo model, all Subsystem blocks have customized icons created using the masking feature.
- Scope blocks display graphic output much as an actual oscilloscope does. Scope blocks are described in detail in the online reference pages.

Other Useful Demos

Other demos illustrate useful modeling concepts. You can access these demos from the Simulink block library window:

1 Type simulink3 in the MATLAB command window. The Simulink block library window appears.

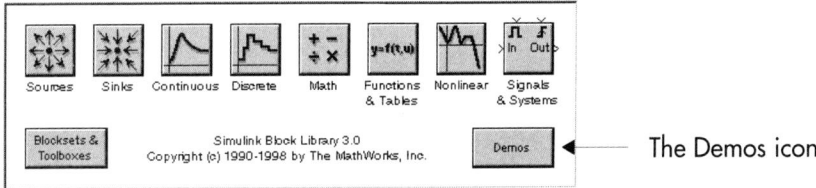
— The Demos icon

2 Double-click on the Demos icon. The MATLAB Demos window appears. This window contains several interesting sample models that illustrate useful Simulink features.

2-5

Building a Simple Model

This example shows you how to build a model using many of the model building commands and actions you will use to build your own models. The instructions for building this model in this section are brief. All of the tasks are described in more detail in the next chapter.

The model integrates a sine wave and displays the result, along with the sine wave. The block diagram of the model looks like this.

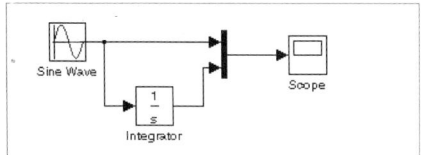

To create the model, first type `simulink` in the MATLAB command window. On Microsoft Windows, the Simulink Library Browser appears.

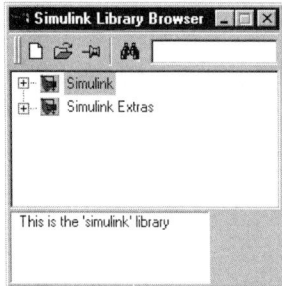

On Linux, the Simulink library block window appears.

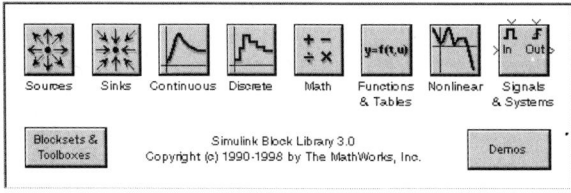

Building a Simple Model

To create a new model on Linux, select **Model** from the **New** submenu of the Simulink library window's **File** menu. To create a new model on Windows, select the **New Model** button on the Library Browser's toolbar.

New Model button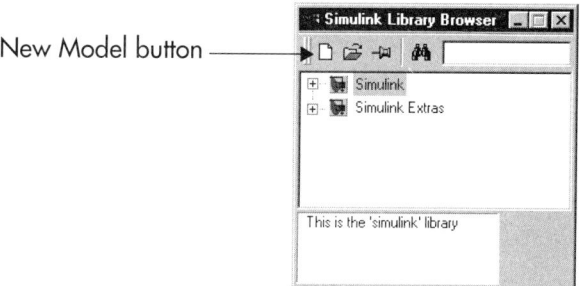

Simulink opens a new model window.

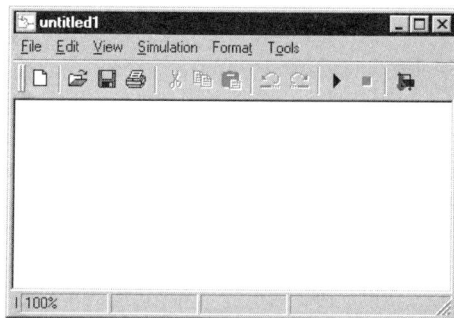

You might want to move the new model window to the right side of your screen so you can see its contents and the contents of block libraries at the same time.

To create this model, you will need to copy blocks into the model from the following Simulink block libraries:

- Sources library (the Sine Wave block)
- Sinks library (the Scope block)
- Continuous library (the Integrator block)
- Signals & Systems library (the Mux block)

You can copy a Sine Wave block from the Sources library, using the Library Browser (Windows only) or the Sources library window (Linux or Windows).

2-7

To copy the Sine Wave block from the Library Browser, first expand the Library Browser tree to display the blocks in the Sources library. Do this by clicking first on the Simulink node to display the Sources node, then on the Sources node to display the Sources library blocks. Finally click on the Sine Wave node to select the Sine Wave block. Here is how the Library Browser should look after you have done this.

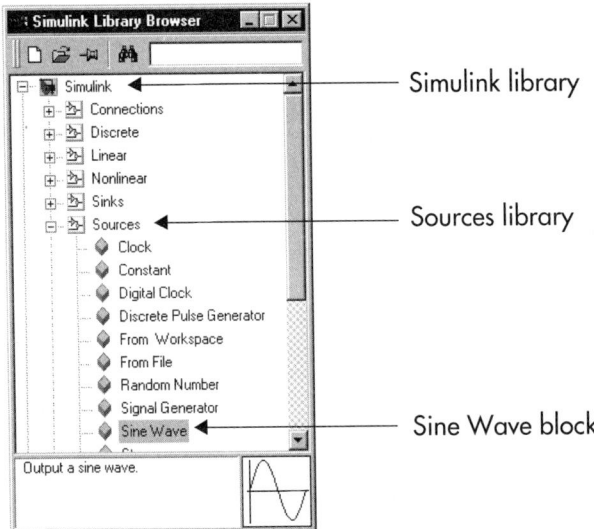

Now drag the Sine Wave node from the browser and drop it in the model window. Simulink creates a copy of the Sine Wave block at the point where you dropped the node icon.

To copy the Sine Wave block from the Sources library window, open the Sources window by double-clicking on the Sources icon in the Simulink library window. (On Windows, you can open the Simulink library window by right-clicking the

Building a Simple Model

Simulink node in the Library Browser and then clicking the resulting **Open Library** button.) Simulink displays the Sources library window.

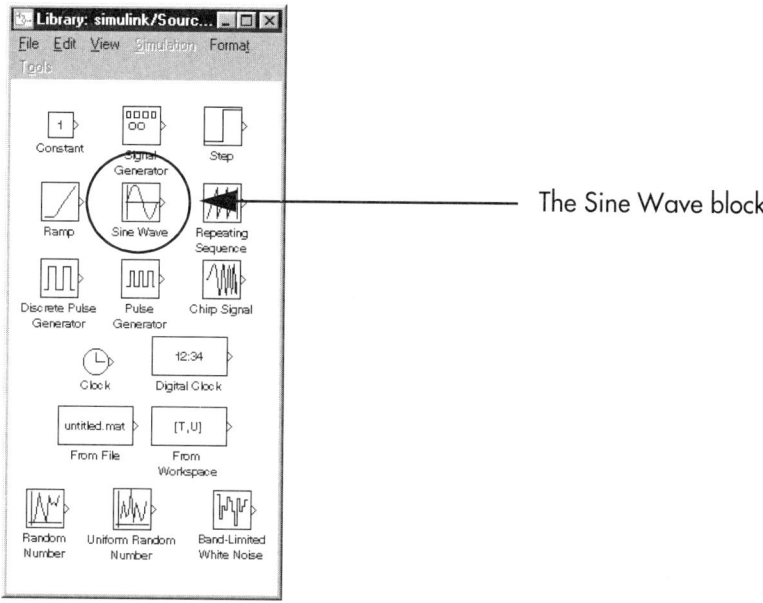

The Sine Wave block

Now drag the Sine Wave block from the Sources window to your model window.

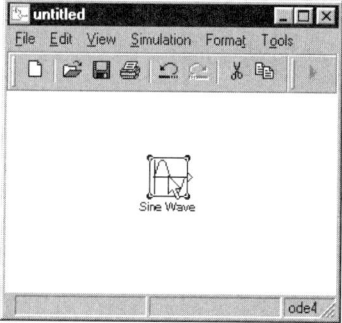

Copy the rest of the blocks in a similar manner from their respective libraries into the model window. You can move a block from one place in the model window to another by dragging the block. You can move a block a short distance by selecting the block, then pressing the arrow keys.

2-9

With all the blocks copied into the model window, the model should look something like this.

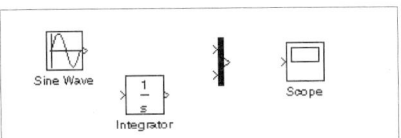

If you examine the block icons, you see an angle bracket on the right of the Sine Wave block and two on the left of the Mux block. The > symbol pointing out of a block is an *output port*; if the symbol points to a block, it is an *input port*. A signal travels out of an output port and into an input port of another block through a connecting line. When the blocks are connected, the port symbols disappear.

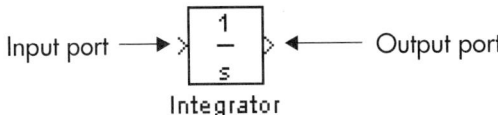

Now it's time to connect the blocks. Connect the Sine Wave block to the top input port of the Mux block. Position the pointer over the output port on the right side of the Sine Wave block. Notice that the cursor shape changes to cross hairs.

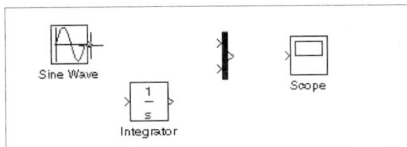

Hold down the mouse button and move the cursor to the top input port of the Mux block. Notice that the line is dashed while the mouse button is down and that the cursor shape changes to double-lined cross hairs as it approaches the Mux block.

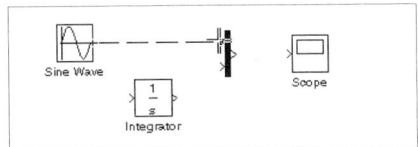

Now release the mouse button. The blocks are connected. You can also connect the line to the block by releasing the mouse button while the pointer is inside the icon. If you do, the line is connected to the input port closest to the cursor's position.

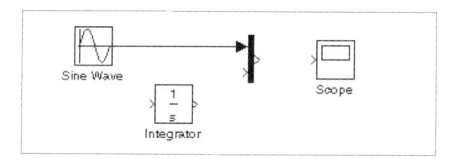

If you look again at the model at the beginning of this section (see "Building a Simple Model" on page 2-6), you'll notice that most of the lines connect output ports of blocks to input ports of other blocks. However, one line connects a *line* to the input port of another block. This line, called a *branch line*, connects the Sine Wave output to the Integrator block, and carries the same signal that passes from the Sine Wave block to the Mux block.

Drawing a branch line is slightly different from drawing the line you just drew. To weld a connection to an existing line, follow these steps:

1 First, position the pointer *on the line* between the Sine Wave and the Mux block.

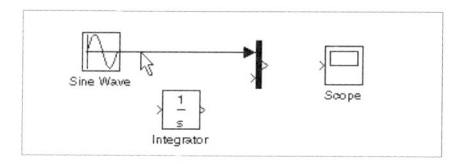

2 Press and hold down the **Ctrl** key. Press the mouse button, then drag the pointer to the Integrator block's input port or over the Integrator block itself.

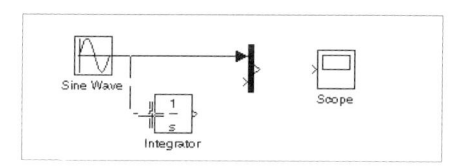

2-11

2 Quick Start

3 Release the mouse button. Simulink draws a line between the starting point and the Integrator block's input port.

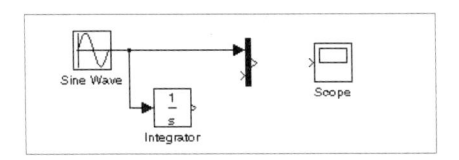

Finish making block connections. When you're done, your model should look something like this.

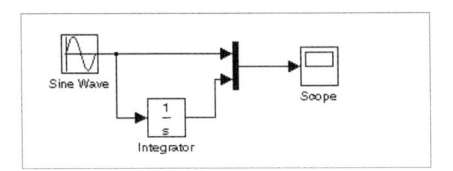

Now, open the Scope block to view the simulation output. Keeping the Scope window open, set up Simulink to run the simulation for 10 seconds. First, set the simulation parameters by choosing **Parameters** from the **Simulation** menu. On the dialog box that appears, notice that the **Stop time** is set to 10.0 (its default value).

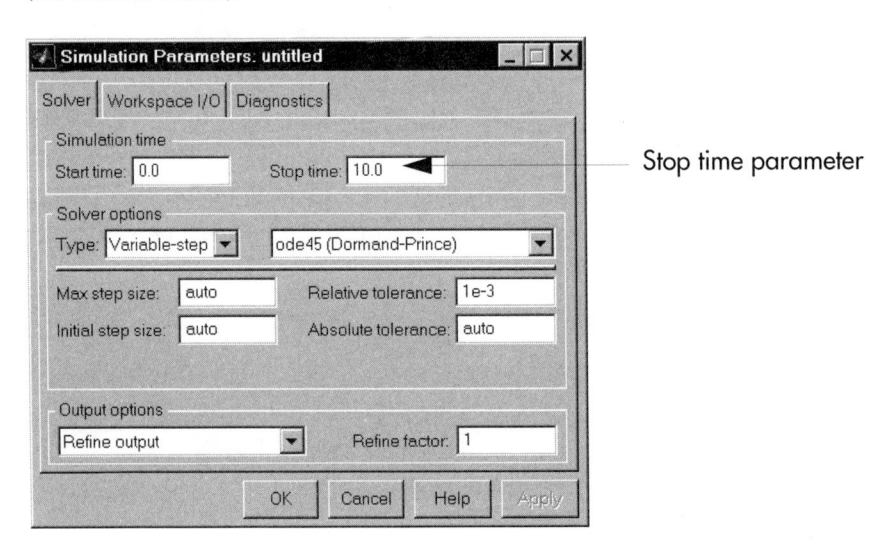

— Stop time parameter

Close the **Simulation Parameters** dialog box by clicking on the **Ok** button. Simulink applies the parameters and closes the dialog box.

Choose **Start** from the **Simulation** menu and watch the traces of the Scope block's input.

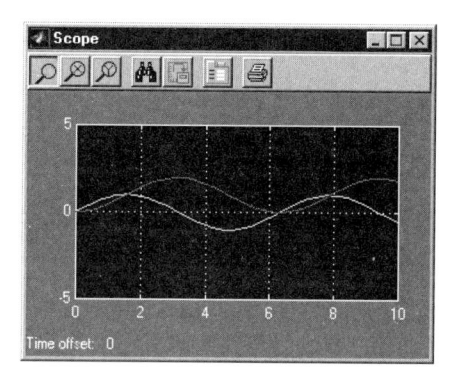

The simulation stops when it reaches the stop time specified in the **Simulation Parameters** dialog box or when you choose **Stop** from the **Simulation** menu.

To save this model, choose **Save** from the **File** menu and enter a filename and location. That file contains the description of the model.

To terminate Simulink and MATLAB, choose **Exit MATLAB** (on a Microsoft Windows system) or **Quit MATLAB** (on a Linux system). You can also type `quit` in the MATLAB command window. If you want to leave Simulink but not terminate MATLAB, just close all Simulink windows.

This exercise shows you how to perform some commonly used model-building tasks. These and other tasks are described in more detail in Chapter 3.

Quick Start

Creating a Model

Starting Simulink	3-2
Selecting Objects	3-7
Blocks	3-9
Libraries	3-21
Lines	3-27
Annotations	3-34
Summary of Mouse and Keyboard Actions	3-35
Creating Subsystems	3-38
Tips for Building Models	3-44
Modeling Equations	3-45
Saving a Model	3-48
Printing a Block Diagram	3-49
The Model Browser	3-53
Ending a Simulink Session	3-57

3 Creating a Model

Starting Simulink

To start Simulink, you must first start MATLAB. Consult your MATLAB documentation for more information. You can then start Simulink in two ways:

- Click on the Simulink icon ![icon] on the MATLAB toolbar.
- Enter the `simulink` command at the MATLAB prompt.

On Microsoft Windows platforms, starting Simulink displays the Simulink Library Browser.

The Library Browser displays a tree-structured view of the Simulink block libraries installed on your system. You can build models by copying blocks from the Library Browser into a model window (this procedure is described later in this chapter).

On Linux platforms, starting Simulink displays the Simulink block library window.

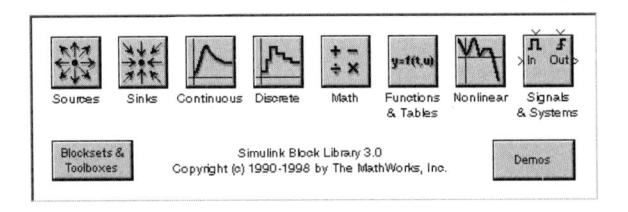

The Simulink library window displays icons representing the block libraries that come with Simulink. You can create models by copying blocks from the library into a model window.

3-2

> **Note** On Windows, you can display the Simulink library window by right-clicking the Simulink node in the Library Browser window.

Creating a New Model

To create a new model, click the **New** button on the Library Browser's toolbar (Windows only) or choose **New** from the library window's **File** menu and select **Model**. You can move the window as you do other windows. Chapter 2 describes how to build a simple model. "Modeling Equations" on page 3–45 describes how to build systems that model equations.

Editing an Existing Model

To edit an existing model diagram, either:

- Choose the **Open** button on the Library Browser's toolbar (Windows only) or the **Open** command from the Simulink library window's **File** menu and then choose or enter the model filename for the model you want to edit.
- Enter the name of the model (without the `.mdl` extension) in the MATLAB command window. The model must be in the current directory or on the path.

Entering Simulink Commands

You run Simulink and work with your model by entering commands. You can enter commands by:

- Selecting items from the Simulink menu bar
- Selecting items from a context-sensitive Simulink menu (Windows only)
- Clicking buttons on the Simulink toolbar (Windows only)
- Entering commands in the MATLAB command window

Using the Simulink Menu Bar to Enter Commands

The Simulink menu bar appears near the top of each model window. The menu commands apply to the contents of that window.

Using Context-Sensitive Menus to Enter Commands

The Windows version of Simulink displays a context-sensitive menu when you click the right mouse button over a model or block library window. The contents of the menu depend on whether a block is selected. If a block is selected, the menu displays commands that apply only to the selected block. If no block is selected, the menu displays commands that apply to a model or library as a whole.

Using the Simulink Toolbar to Enter Commands

Model windows in the Windows version of Simulink optionally display a toolbar beneath the Simulink menu bar. To display the toolbar, check the **Toolbar** option on the Simulink **View** menu.

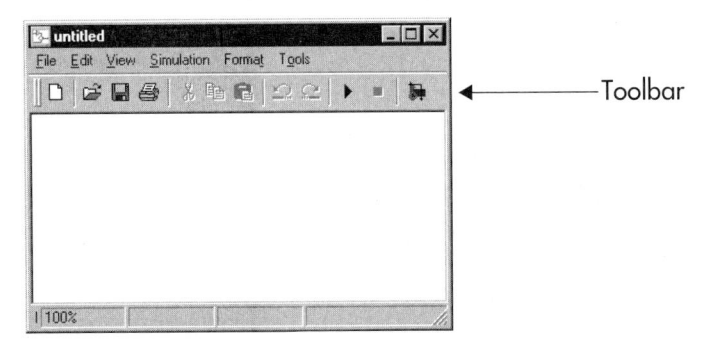

The toolbar contains buttons corresponding to frequently used Simulink commands, such as those for opening, running, and closing models. You can run such commands by clicking on the corresponding button. For example, to open a Simulink model, click on the button containing an open folder icon. You can determine which command a button executes by moving the mouse pointer over the button. A small window appears containing text that describes the button. The window is called a tooltip. Each button on the toolbar displays a tooltip when the mouse pointer hovers over it. You can hide the toolbar by unchecking the **Toolbar** option on the Simulink **View** menu.

Using the MATLAB Window to Enter Commands

When you run a simulation and analyze its results, you can enter MATLAB commands in the MATLAB command window. Running a simulation is discussed in Chapter 4, and analyzing simulation results is discussed in Chapter 5.

Undoing a Command

You can cancel the effects of up to 101 consecutive operations by choosing **Undo** from the **Edit** menu. You can undo these operations:

- Adding or deleting a block
- Adding or deleting a line
- Adding or deleting a model annotation
- Editing a block name

You can reverse the effects of an **Undo** command by choosing **Redo** from the **Edit** menu.

Simulink Windows

Simulink uses separate windows to display a block library browser, a block library, a model, and graphical (scope) simulation output. These windows are not MATLAB figure windows and cannot be manipulated using Handle Graphics® commands.

Simulink windows are sized to accommodate the most common screen resolutions available. If you have a monitor with exceptionally high or low resolution, you may find the window sizes too small or too large. If this is the case, resize the window and save the model to preserve the new window dimensions.

Status Bar

The Windows version of Simulink displays a status bar at the bottom of each model and library window.

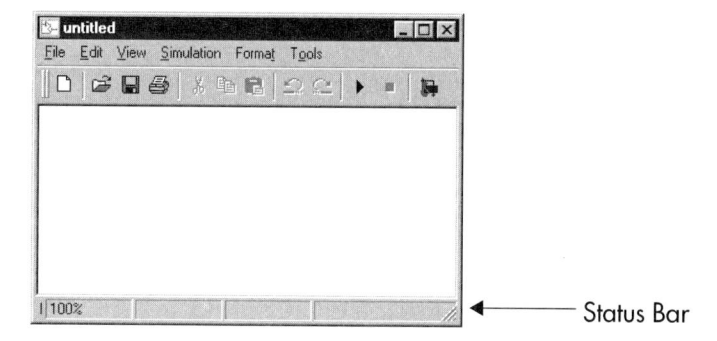

When a simulation is running, the status bar displays the status of the simulation, including the current simulation time and the name of the current solver. You can display or hide the status bar by checking or unchecking the **Status Bar** item on the Simulink **View** menu.

Zooming Block Diagrams

Simulink allows you to enlarge or shrink the view of the block diagram in the current Simulink window. To zoom a view:

- Select **Zoom In** from the **View** menu (or type r) to enlarge the view.
- Select **Zoom Out** from the **View** menu (or type v) to shrink the view.
- Select **Fit System to View** from the **View** menu (or press the space bar) to fit the diagram to the view.
- Select **Normal** from the **View** menu to view the diagram at actual size.

By default, Simulink fits a block diagram to view when you open the diagram either in the model browser's content pane or in a separate window. If you change a diagram's zoom setting, Simulink saves the setting when you close the diagram and restores the setting the next time you open the diagram. If you want to restore the default behavior, choose **Fit System to View** from the **View** menu the next time you open the diagram.

Selecting Objects

Many model building actions, such as copying a block or deleting a line, require that you first select one or more blocks and lines (objects).

Selecting One Object

To select an object, click on it. Small black square "handles" appear at the corners of a selected block and near the end points of a selected line. For example, the figure below shows a selected Sine Wave block and a selected line.

When you select an object by clicking on it, any other selected objects become deselected.

Selecting More than One Object

You can select more than one object either by selecting objects one at a time, by selecting objects located near each other using a bounding box, or by selecting the entire model.

Selecting Multiple Objects One at a Time

To select more than one object by selecting each object individually, hold down the **Shift** key and click on each object to be selected. To deselect a selected object, click on the object again while holding down the **Shift** key.

Selecting Multiple Objects Using a Bounding Box

An easy way to select more than one object in the same area of the window is to draw a bounding box around the objects.

3 Creating a Model

1 Define the starting corner of a bounding box by positioning the pointer at one corner of the box, then pressing and holding down the mouse button. Notice the shape of the cursor.

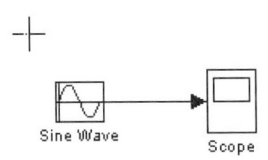

2 Drag the pointer to the opposite corner of the box. A dotted rectangle encloses the selected blocks and lines.

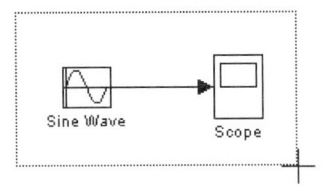

3 Release the mouse button. All blocks and lines at least partially enclosed by the bounding box are selected.

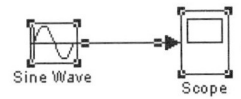

Selecting the Entire Model

To select all objects in the active window, choose **Select All** from the **Edit** menu. You cannot create a subsystem by selecting blocks and lines in this way; for more information, see "Creating Subsystems" on page 3–38.

Blocks

Blocks are the elements from which Simulink models are built. You can model virtually any dynamic system by creating and interconnecting blocks in appropriate ways. This section discusses how to use blocks to build models of dynamic systems.

Block Data Tips

On Microsoft Windows, Simulink displays information about a block in a pop-up window when you allow the pointer to hover over the block in the diagram view. To disable this feature or control what information a data tip includes, select **Block Data Tips** from the Simulink **View** menu.

Virtual Blocks

When creating models, you need to be aware that Simulink blocks fall into two basic categories: nonvirtual and virtual blocks. Nonvirtual blocks play an active role in the simulation of a system. If you add or remove a nonvirtual block, you change the model's behavior. Virtual blocks, by contrast, play no active role in the simulation. They simply help to organize a model graphically. Some Simulink blocks can be virtual in some circumstances and nonvirtual in others. Such blocks are called conditionally virtual blocks. The following table lists Simulink's virtual and conditionally virtual blocks.

Table 3-1: Virtual Blocks

Block Name	Condition Under Which Block Will Be Virtual
Bus Selector	Always virtual.
Data Store Memory	Always virtual.
Demux	Always virtual.
Enable Port	Always virtual.
From	Always virtual.
Goto	Always virtual.
Goto Tag Visibility	Always virtual.

Table 3-1: Virtual Blocks (Continued)

Block Name	Condition Under Which Block Will Be Virtual
Ground	Always virtual.
Inport	Always virtual *unless* the block resides in a conditionally executed subsystem *and* has a direct connection to an outport block.
Mux	Always virtual.
Outport	Virtual if the block resides within any subsystem block (conditional or not), and does *not* reside in the root (top-level) Simulink window.
Selector	Always virtual.
Subsystem	Virtual if the block is not conditionally executed.
Terminator	Always virtual.
Test Point	Always virtual.
Trigger Port	Virtual if the outport port is not present.

Copying and Moving Blocks from One Window to Another

As you build your model, you often copy blocks from Simulink block libraries or other libraries or models into your model window. To do this, follow these steps:

1 Open the appropriate block library or model window.

2 Drag the block you want to copy into the target model window. To drag a block, position the cursor over the block icon, then press and hold down the mouse button. Move the cursor into the target window, then release the mouse button.

You can also drag blocks from the Simulink Library Browser into a model window. See "Browsing Block Libraries" on page 3-24 for more information.

> **Note** Simulink hides the names of Sum, Mux, Demux, and Bus Selector blocks when you copy them from the Simulink block library to a model. This is done to avoid unnecessarily cluttering the model diagram. (The shapes of these blocks clearly indicates their respective functions.)

You can also copy blocks by using the **Copy** and **Paste** commands from the **Edit** menu:

1 Select the block you want to copy.

2 Choose **Copy** from the **Edit** menu.

3 Make the target model window the active window.

4 Choose **Paste** from the **Edit** menu.

Simulink assigns a name to each copied block. If it is the first block of its type in the model, its name is the same as its name in the source window. For example, if you copy the Gain block from the Math library into your model window, the name of the new block is Gain. If your model already contains a block named Gain, Simulink adds a sequence number to the block name (for example, Gain1, Gain2). You can rename blocks; see "Manipulating Block Names" on page 3–16.

When you copy a block, the new block inherits all the original block's parameter values.

Simulink uses an invisible five-pixel grid to simplify the alignment of blocks. All blocks within a model snap to a line on the grid. You can move a block slightly up, down, left, or right by selecting the block and pressing the arrow keys.

You can display the grid in the model window by typing the following command in the MATLAB window.

```
set_param('<model name>','showgrid','on')
```

To change the grid spacing, type

```
set_param('<model name>','gridspacing',<number of pixels>)
```

For example, to change the grid spacing to 20 pixels, type

```
set_param('<model name>','gridspacing',20)
```

For either of the above commands, you can also select the model, and then type gcs instead of <model name>.

You can copy or move blocks to compatible applications (such as word processing programs) using the **Copy**, **Cut**, and **Paste** commands. These commands copy only the graphic representation of the blocks, not their parameters.

Moving blocks from one window to another is similar to copying blocks, except that you hold down the **Shift** key while you select the blocks.

You can use the **Undo** command from the **Edit** menu to remove an added block.

Moving Blocks in a Model

To move a single block from one place to another in a model window, drag the block to a new location. Simulink automatically repositions lines connected to the moved block.

To move more than one block, including connecting lines:

1 Select the blocks and lines. If you need information about how to select more than one block, see "Selecting More than One Object" on page 3–7.

2 Drag the objects to their new location and release the mouse button.

Duplicating Blocks in a Model

You can duplicate blocks in a model as follows. While holding down the **Ctrl** key, select the block with the left mouse button, then drag it to a new location. You can also do this by dragging the block using the right mouse button. Duplicated blocks have the same parameter values as the original blocks. Sequence numbers are added to the new block names.

Specifying Block Parameters

The Simulink user interface lets you assign values to block parameters. Some block parameters are common to all blocks. Use the **Block Properties** dialog box to set these parameters. To display the dialog box, select the block whose properties you want to set. Then select **Block Properties...** from Simulink's **Edit** menu. See "Block Properties Dialog Box" on page 3-13 for more information.

Other block parameters are specific to particular blocks. Use a block's block-specific parameter dialog to set these parameters. Double-click on the block to open its dialog box. You can accept the displayed values or change them. You can also use the set_param command to change block parameters. See set_param in the online documentation for details.

Some block dialogs allow you to specify a data type for some or all of their parameters. The online reference material that describes each block shows the dialog box and describes the block parameters.

Block Properties Dialog Box

The **Block Properties** dialog box lets you set some common block parameters.

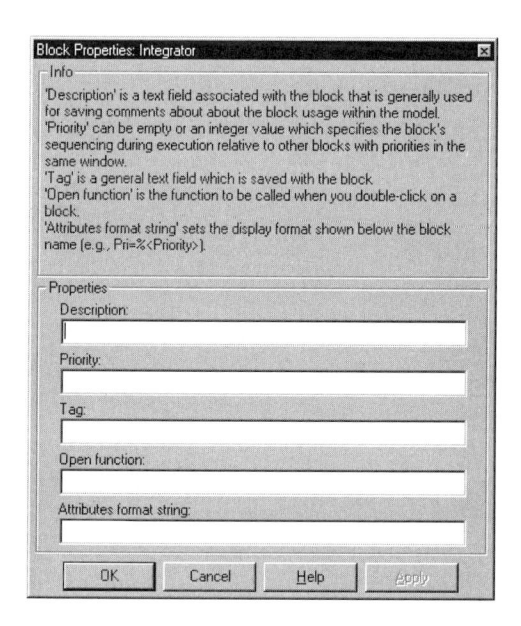

The dialog box contains the following fields:

Description
Brief description of the block's purpose.

Priority

Execution priority of this block relative to other blocks in the model. See "Assigning Block Priorities" on page 3-19 for more information.

Tag

A general text field that is saved with the block.

Open Function

MATLAB (m-) function to be called when a user opens this block.

Attributes Format String

Current value of the block's `AttributesFormatString` parameter. This parameter specifies which parameters to display beneath a block's icon. The attributes format string can be any text string with embedded parameter names. An embedded parameter name is a parameter name preceded by `%<` and followed by `>`, for example, `%<priority>`. Simulink displays the attributes format string beneath the block's icon, replacing each parameter name with the corresponding parameter value. You can use line feed characters (`\n`) to display each parameter on a separate line. For example, specifying the attributes format string

```
pri=%<priority>\ngain=%<Gain>
```

for a Gain block displays

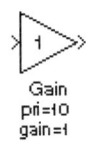

```
   Gain
   pri=10
   gain=1
```

If a parameter's value is not a string or an integer, Simulink displays `N/S` (not supported) for the parameter's value. If the parameter name is invalid, Simulink displays "???".

Deleting Blocks

To delete one or more blocks, select the blocks to be deleted and press the **Delete** or **Backspace** key. You can also choose **Clear** or **Cut** from the **Edit** menu. The **Cut** command writes the blocks into the clipboard, which enables you to paste them into a model. Using the **Delete** or **Backspace** key or the **Clear** command does not enable you to paste the block later.

You can use the **Undo** command from the **Edit** menu to replace a deleted block.

Changing the Orientation of Blocks

By default, signals flow through a block from left to right. Input ports are on the left, and output ports are on the right. You can change the orientation of a block by choosing one of these commands from the **Format** menu:

- The **Flip Block** command rotates the block 180 degrees.
- The **Rotate Block** command rotates a block clockwise 90 degrees.

The figure below shows how Simulink orders ports after changing the orientation of a block using the **Rotate Block** and **Flip Block** menu items. The text in the blocks shows their orientation.

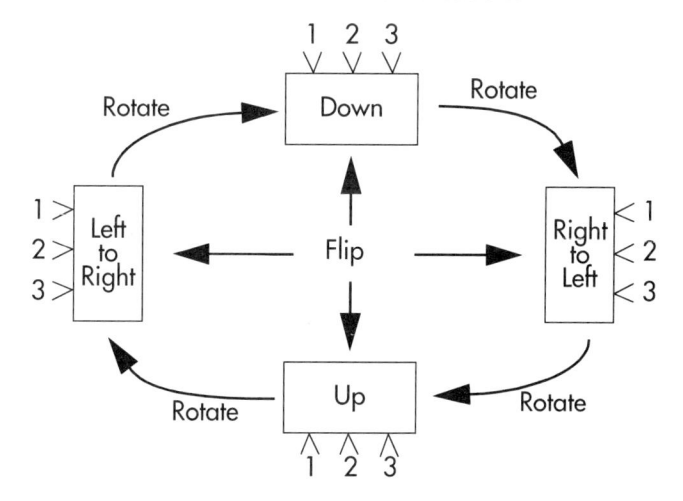

Resizing Blocks

To change the size of a block, select it, then drag any of its selection handles. While you hold down the mouse button, a dotted rectangle shows the new block size. When you release the mouse button, the block is resized.

For example, the figure below shows a Signal Generator block being resized. The lower-right handle was selected and dragged to the cursor position. When the mouse button is released, the block takes its new size. This figure shows a block being resized.

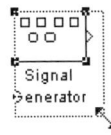

Manipulating Block Names

All block names in a model must be unique and must contain at least one character. By default, block names appear below blocks whose ports are on the sides, and to the left of blocks whose ports are on the top and bottom, as this figure shows.

Changing Block Names

You can edit a block name in one of these ways:

- To replace the block name on a Microsoft Windows or Linux system, click on the block name, then double-click or drag the cursor to select the entire name. Then, enter the new name.
- To insert characters, click between two characters to position the insertion point, then insert text.
- To replace characters, drag the mouse to select a range of text to replace, then enter the new text.

When you click the pointer someplace else in the model or take any other action, the name is accepted or rejected. If you try to change the name of a block to a name that already exists or to a name with no characters, Simulink displays an error message.

You can modify the font used in a block name by selecting the block, then choosing the **Font** menu item from the **Format** menu. Select a font from the **Set Font** dialog box. This procedure also changes the font of text on the block icon.

You can cancel edits to a block name by choosing **Undo** from the **Edit** menu.

> **Note** If you change the name of a library block, all links to that block will become unresolved.

Changing the Location of a Block Name

You can change the location of the name of a selected block in two ways:

- By dragging the block name to the opposite side of the block
- By choosing the **Flip Name** command from the **Format** menu. This command changes the location of the block name to the opposite side of the block.

For more information about block orientation, see "Changing the Orientation of Blocks" on page 3–15.

Changing Whether a Block Name Appears

To change whether the name of a selected block is displayed, choose a menu item from the **Format** menu:

- The **Hide Name** menu item hides a visible block name. When you select **Hide Name**, it changes to **Show Name** when that block is selected.
- The **Show Name** menu item shows a hidden block name.

Displaying Parameters Beneath a Block's Icon

You can cause Simulink to display one or more of a block's parameters beneath the block's icon in a block diagram. You specify the parameters to be displayed in the following ways:

- By entering an attributes format string in the **Attributes format string** field of the block's **Block Properties** dialog box (see "Block Properties Dialog Box" on page 3-13)
- By setting the value of the block's AttributesFormatString property to the format string, using set_param (see set_param in the online documentation)

Disconnecting Blocks

To disconnect a block from its connecting lines, hold down the **Shift** key, then drag the block to a new location.

Vector Input and Output

Almost all Simulink blocks accept scalar or vector inputs, generate scalar or vector outputs, and allow you to provide scalar or vector parameters. These blocks are referred to in this manual as being *vectorized*.

You can determine which lines in a model carry vector signals by choosing **Wide Vector Lines** from the **Format** menu. When this option is selected, lines that carry vectors are drawn thicker than lines that carry scalars. The figures in the next section show scalar and vector lines.

If you change your model after choosing **Wide Vector Lines**, you must explicitly update the display by choosing **Update Diagram** from the **Edit** menu. Starting the simulation also updates the block diagram display.

Block descriptions in the online documentation discuss the characteristics of block inputs, outputs, and parameters.

Scalar Expansion of Inputs and Parameters

Scalar expansion is the conversion of a scalar value into a vector of identical elements. Simulink applies scalar expansion to inputs and/or parameters for most blocks. Block descriptions in the online documentation indicate whether Simulink applies scalar expansion to a block's inputs and parameters.

Scalar Expansion of Inputs

When using blocks with more than one input port (such as the Sum or Relational Operator block), you can mix vector and scalar inputs. When you do this, the scalar inputs are expanded into vectors of identical elements whose widths are equal to the width of the vector inputs. (If more than one block input is a vector, they must have the same number of elements.)

This model adds scalar and vector inputs. The input from block Constant1 is scalar expanded to match the size of the vector input from the Constant block. The input is expanded to the vector [3 3 3].

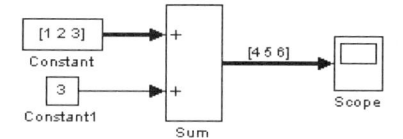

Scalar Expansion of Parameters

You can specify the parameters for vectorized blocks as either vectors or scalars. When you specify vector parameters, each parameter element is associated with the corresponding element in the input vector(s). When you specify scalar parameters, Simulink applies scalar expansion to convert them automatically into appropriately sized vectors.

This example shows that a scalar parameter (the Gain) is expanded to a vector of identically valued elements to match the size of the block input, a three-element vector.

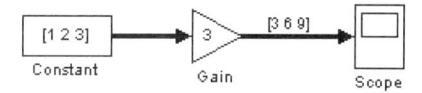

Assigning Block Priorities

You can assign evaluation priorities to nonvirtual blocks in a model. Higher priority blocks evaluate before lower priority blocks, though not necessarily before blocks that have no assigned priority.

You can assign block priorities interactively or programmatically. To set priorities programmatically, use the command

```
set_param(b,'Priority','n')
```

where b is a block path and n is any valid integer. (Negative numbers and 0 are valid priority values.) The lower the number, the higher the priority; that is, 2 is higher priority than 3. To set a block's priority interactively, enter the priority in the **Priority** field of the block's **Block Properties** dialog box (see "Block Properties Dialog Box" on page 3-13).

3-19

Using Drop Shadows

You can add a drop shadow to a block by selecting the block, then choosing **Show Drop Shadow** from the **Format** menu. When you select a block with a drop shadow, the menu item changes to **Hide Drop Shadow**. The figure below shows a Subsystem block with a drop shadow.

Libraries

Libraries enable users to copy blocks into their models from external libraries and automatically update the copied blocks when the source blocks change. Using libraries allows users who develop their own block libraries, or who use those provided by others (such as blocksets), to ensure that their models automatically include the most recent versions of these blocks.

Terminology

It is important to understand the terminology used with this feature.

Library – A collection of library blocks. A library must be explicitly created using **New Library** from the **File** menu.

Library block – A block in a library.

Reference block – A copy of a library block.

Link – The connection between the reference block and its library block that allows Simulink to update the reference block when the library block changes.

Copy – The operation that creates a reference block from either a library block or another reference block.

This figure illustrates this terminology.

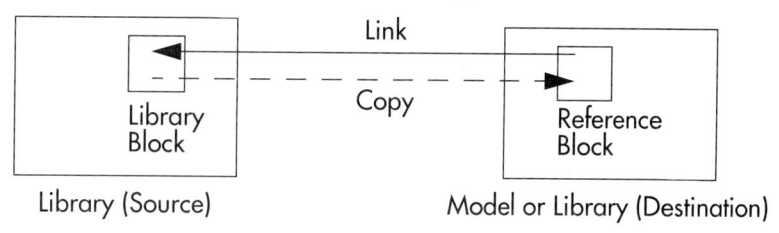

Copying a Library Block into a Model

You can copy a block from a library into a model by copying and pasting or dragging the block from the library window to the model window (see "Copying and Moving Blocks from One Window to Another" on page 3-10) or by dragging the block from the Library Browser (see "Browsing Block Libraries" on page 3-24) into the model window.

When you copy a library block into a model or another library, Simulink creates a link to the library block. The reference block is a copy of the library block. You can modify block parameters in the reference block but you cannot mask the block or, if it is masked, edit the mask. Also, you cannot set callback parameters for a reference block. If you look under the mask of a reference block, Simulink displays the underlying system for the library block.

The library and reference blocks are linked *by name*; that is, the reference block is linked to the specific block and library whose names are in effect at the time the copy is made.

If Simulink is unable to find either the library block or the source library on your MATLAB path when it attempts to update the reference block, the link becomes *unresolved*. Simulink issues an error message and displays these blocks using red dashed lines. The error message is

```
Failed to find block "source-block-name"
in library "source-library-name"
referenced by block
"reference-block-path".
```

The unresolved reference block is displayed like this (colored red).

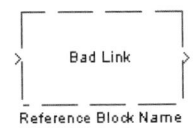

To fix a bad link, you must either:

- Delete the unlinked reference block and copy the library block back into your model.
- Add the directory that contains the required library to the MATLAB path and select **Update Diagram** from the **Edit** menu.
- Double-click on the reference block. On the dialog box that appears, correct the pathname and click on **Apply** or **Close**.

All blocks have a `LinkStatus` parameter that indicates whether the block is a reference block. The parameter can have these values:

- 'none' indicates that the block is not a reference block.
- 'resolved' indicates that the block is a reference block and that the link is resolved.
- 'unresolved' indicates that the block is a reference block but that the link is unresolved.

Updating a Linked Block

Simulink updates out-of-date reference blocks in a model or library at these times:

- When the model or library is loaded
- When you select **Update Diagram** from the **Edit** menu or run the simulation
- When you query the LinkStatus parameter of a block using the get_param command (see "Getting Information About Library Blocks" on page 3-24)
- When you use the find_system command

Breaking a Link to a Library Block

You can break the link between a reference block and its library block to cause the reference block to become a simple copy of the library block, unlinked to the library block. Changes to the library block no longer affect the block. Breaking links to library blocks enables you to transport a model as a stand-alone model, without the libraries.

To break the link between a reference block and its library block, select the block, then choose **Break Library Link** from the **Edit** menu. You can also break the link between a reference block and its library block from the command line by changing the value of the LinkStatus parameter to 'none' using this command.

```
set_param('refblock', 'LinkStatus', 'none')
```

You can save a system and break all links between reference blocks and library blocks using this command.

```
save_system('sys', 'newname', 'BreakLinks')
```

Finding the Library Block for a Reference Block

To find the source library and block linked to a reference block, select the reference block, then choose **Go To Library Link** from the **Edit** menu. If the library is open, Simulink selects the library block (displaying selection handles on the block) and makes the source library the active window. If the library is not open, Simulink opens it and selects the library block.

Getting Information About Library Blocks

Use the libinfo command to get information about reference blocks in a system. The format for the command is

```
libdata = libinfo(sys)
```

where sys is the name of the system. The command returns a structure of size n-by-1, where n is the number of library blocks in sys. Each element of the structure has four fields:

- Block, the block path
- Library, the library name
- ReferenceBlock, the reference block path
- LinkStatus, the link status, either 'resolved' or 'unresolved'

Browsing Block Libraries

The Library Browser lets you quickly locate and copy library blocks into a model.

Note The Library Browser is available only on Microsoft Windows platforms.

You can locate blocks either by navigating the Library Browser's library tree or by using the Library Browser's search facility.

Navigating the Library Tree

The library tree displays a list of all the block libraries installed on the system. You can view or hide the contents of libraries by expanding or collapsing the tree using the mouse or keyboard. To expand/collapse the tree, click the +/- buttons next to library entries or select an entry and press the +/- or right/left arrow key on your keyboard. Use the up/down arrow keys to move up or down the tree.

Searching Libraries

To find a particular block, enter the block's name in the edit field next to the Library Browser's **Find** button and then click the **Find** button.

Opening a Library

To open a library, right-click the library's entry in the browser. Simulink displays an **Open Library** button. Select the **Open Library** button to open the library.

Creating and Opening Models

To create a model, select the **New** button on the Library Browser's toolbar. To open an existing model, select the **Open** button on the toolbar.

Copying Blocks

To copy a block from the Library Browser into a model, select the block in the browser, drag the selected block into the model window, and drop it where you want to create the copy.

Displaying Help on a Block

To display help on a block, right-click the block in the Library Browser and select the button that subsequently pops up.

Pinning the Library Browser

To keep the Library Browser above all other windows on your desktop, select the **PushPin** button on the browser's toolbar.

Lines

Lines carry signals. Each line can carry a scalar or vector signal. A line can connect the output port of one block with the input port of another block. A line can also connect the output port of one block with input ports of many blocks by using branch lines.

Drawing a Line Between Blocks

To connect the output port of one block to the input port of another block:

1 Position the cursor over the first block's output port. It is not necessary to position the cursor precisely on the port. The cursor shape changes to a cross hair.

2 Press and hold down the mouse button.

3 Drag the pointer to the second block's input port. You can position the cursor on or near the port, or in the block. If you position the cursor in the block, the line is connected to the closest input port. The cursor shape changes to a double cross hair.

4 Release the mouse button. Simulink replaces the port symbols by a connecting line with an arrow showing the direction of the signal flow. You can create lines either from output to input, or from input to output. The arrow is drawn at the appropriate input port, and the signal is the same.

Simulink draws connecting lines using horizontal and vertical line segments. To draw a diagonal line, hold down the **Shift** key while drawing the line.

Drawing a Branch Line

A *branch line* is a line that starts from an existing line and carries its signal to the input port of a block. Both the existing line and the branch line carry the same signal. Using branch lines enables you to cause one signal to be carried to more than one block.

In this example, the output of the Product block goes to both the Scope block and the To Workspace block.

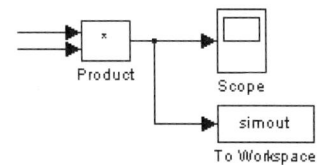

To add a branch line, follow these steps:

1 Position the pointer on the line where you want the branch line to start.

2 While holding down the **Ctrl** key, press and hold down the left mouse button.

3 Drag the pointer to the input port of the target block, then release the mouse button and the **Ctrl** key.

You can also use the right mouse button instead of holding down the left mouse button and the **Ctrl** key.

Drawing a Line Segment

You may want to draw a line with segments exactly where you want them instead of where Simulink draws them. Or, you might want to draw a line before you copy the block to which the line is connected. You can do either by drawing line segments.

To draw a line segment, you draw a line that ends in an unoccupied area of the diagram. An arrow appears on the unconnected end of the line. To add another line segment, position the cursor over the end of the segment and draw another segment. Simulink draws the segments as horizontal and vertical lines. To draw diagonal line segments, hold down the **Shift** key while you draw the lines.

Moving a Line Segment

To move a line segment, follow these steps:

1 Position the pointer on the segment you want to move.

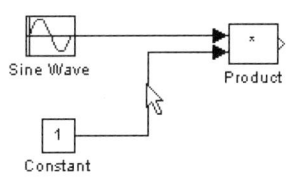

2 Press and hold down the left mouse button.

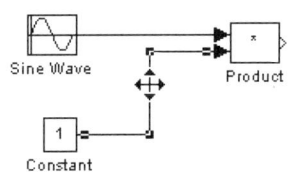

3 Drag the pointer to the desired location.

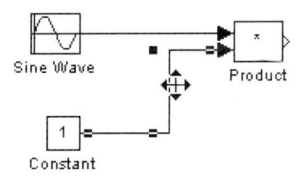

4 Release the mouse button.

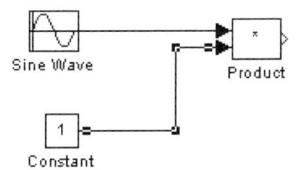

You cannot move the segments that are connected directly to block ports.

Dividing a Line into Segments

You can divide a line segment into two segments, leaving the ends of the line in their original locations. Simulink creates line segments and a vertex that joins them. To divide a line into segments, follow these steps:

3-29

3 Creating a Model

1 Select the line.

2 Position the pointer on the line where you want the vertex.

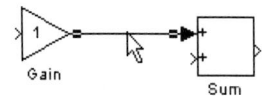

3 While holding down the **Shift** key, press and hold down the mouse button. The cursor shape changes to a circle that encloses the new vertex.

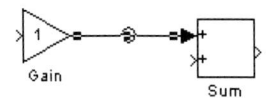

4 Drag the pointer to the desired location.

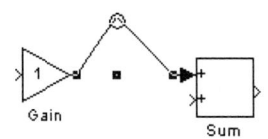

5 Release the mouse button and the **Shift** key.

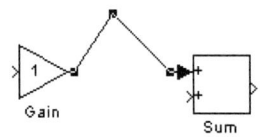

Moving a Line Vertex

To move a vertex of a line, follow these steps:

1 Position the pointer on the vertex, then press and hold down the mouse button. The cursor changes to a circle that encloses the vertex.

2 Drag the pointer to the desired location.

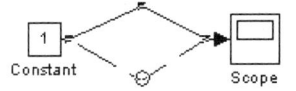

3 Release the mouse button.

Displaying Line Widths

You can display the widths of vector lines in a model by turning on **Vector Line Widths** from the **Format** menu. Simulink indicates the width of each signal at the block that originates the signal and the block that receives it. You can cause Simulink to use a thick line to display vector lines by selecting **Wide Vector Lines** from the **Format** menu.

When you start a simulation or update the diagram and Simulink detects a mismatch of input and output ports, it displays an error message and shows line widths in the model.

Inserting Blocks in a Line

You can insert a block in a line by dropping the block on the line. Simulink inserts the block for you at the point where you drop the block. The block that you insert can have only one input and one output.

3 Creating a Model

To insert a block in a line:

1 Position the pointer over the block and press the left mouse button.

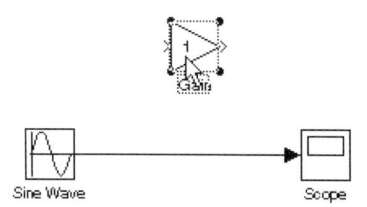

2 Drag the block over the line in which you want to insert the block.

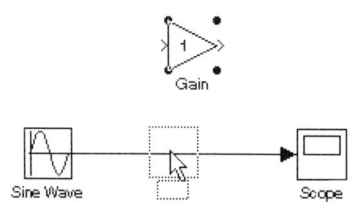

3 Release the mouse button to drop the block on the line. Simulink inserts the block where you dropped it.

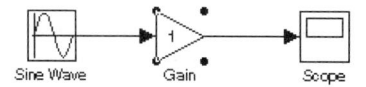

Signal Labels

You can label signals to annotate your model. Labels can appear above or below horizontal lines or line segments, and left or right of vertical lines or line segments. Labels can appear at either end, at the center, or in any combination of these locations.

Using Signal Labels

To create a signal label, double-click on the line segment and type the label at the insertion point. When you click on another part of the model, the label fixes its location.

Note When you create a signal label, take care to double-click *on* the line. If you click in an unoccupied area close to the line, you will create a model annotation instead.

To move a signal label, drag the label to a new location on the line. When you release the mouse button, the label fixes its position near the line.

To copy a signal label, hold down the **Ctrl** key while dragging the label to another location on the line. When you release the mouse button, the label appears in both the original and the new locations.

To edit a signal label, select it:

- To replace the label, click on the label, then double-click or drag the cursor to select the entire label. Then, enter the new label.
- To insert characters, click between two characters to position the insertion point, then insert text.
- To replace characters, drag the mouse to select a range of text to replace, then enter the new text.

To delete all occurrences of a signal label, delete all the characters in the label. When you click outside the label, the labels are deleted. To delete a single occurrence of the label, hold down the **Shift** key while you select the label, then press the **Delete** or **Backspace** key.

To change the font of a signal label, select the signal, choose **Font** from the **Format** menu, then select a font from the **Set Font** dialog box.

Annotations

Annotations provide textual information about a model. You can add an annotation to any unoccupied area of your block diagram.

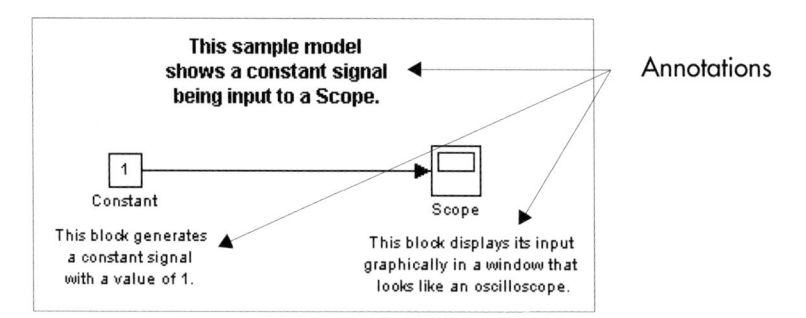

[Figure: A sample model diagram showing a Constant block connected to a Scope block, with annotations labeled "This sample model shows a constant signal being input to a Scope.", "This block generates a constant signal with a value of 1.", and "This block displays its input graphically in a window that looks like an oscilloscope." Arrows point from the label "Annotations" to these text elements.]

To create a model annotation, double-click on an unoccupied area of the block diagram. A small rectangle appears and the cursor changes to an insertion point. Start typing the annotation contents. Each line is centered within the rectangle that surrounds the annotation.

To move an annotation, drag it to a new location.

To edit an annotation, select it:

- To replace the annotation on a Microsoft Windows or Linux system, click on the annotation, then double-click or drag the cursor to select it. Then, enter the new annotation.
- To insert characters, click between two characters to position the insertion point, then insert text.
- To replace characters, drag the mouse to select a range of text to replace, then enter the new text.

To delete an annotation, hold down the **Shift** key while you select the annotation, then press the **Delete** or **Backspace** key.

To change the font of all or part of an annotation, select the text in the annotation you want to change, then choose **Font** from the **Format** menu. Select a font and size from the dialog box.

Summary of Mouse and Keyboard Actions

These tables summarize the use of the mouse and keyboard to manipulate blocks, lines, and signal labels. LMB means press the left mouse button; CMB, the center mouse button; and RMB, the right mouse button.

The first table lists mouse and keyboard actions that apply to blocks.

Table 3-2: Manipulating Blocks

Task	Microsoft Windows	Linux
Select one block	LMB	LMB
Select multiple blocks	**Shift** + LMB	**Shift** + LMB; or CMB alone
Copy block from another window	Drag block	Drag block
Move block	Drag block	Drag block
Duplicate block	**Ctrl** + LMB and drag; or RMB and drag	**Ctrl** + LMB and drag; or RMB and drag
Connect blocks	LMB	LMB
Disconnect block	**Shift** + drag block	**Shift** + drag block; or CMB and drag

The next table lists mouse and keyboard actions that apply to lines.

Table 3-3: Manipulating Lines

Task	Microsoft Windows	Linux
Select one line	LMB	LMB
Select multiple lines	**Shift** + LMB	**Shift** + LMB; or CMB alone
Draw branch line	**Ctrl** + drag line; or **RMB** and drag line	**Ctrl** + drag line; or RMB + drag line

Table 3-3: Manipulating Lines (Continued)

Task	Microsoft Windows	Linux
Route lines around blocks	**Shift** + draw line segments	**Shift** + draw line segments; or CMB and draw segments
Move line segment	Drag segment	Drag segment
Move vertex	Drag vertex	Drag vertex
Create line segments	**Shift** + drag line	**Shift** + drag line; or CMB + drag line

The next table lists mouse and keyboard actions that apply to signal labels.

Table 3-4: Manipulating Signal Labels

Action	Microsoft Windows	Linux
Create signal label	Double-click on line, then type label	Double-click on line, then type label
Copy signal label	**Ctrl** + drag label	**Ctrl** + drag label
Move signal label	Drag label	Drag label
Edit signal label	Click in label, then edit	Click in label, then edit
Delete signal label	**Shift** + click on label, then press **Delete**	**Shift** + click on label, then press **Delete**

The next table lists mouse and keyboard actions that apply to annotations.

Table 3-5: Manipulating Annotations

Action	Microsoft Windows	Linux
Create annotation	Double-click in diagram, then type text	Double-click in diagram, then type text
Copy annotation	**Ctrl** + drag label	**Ctrl** + drag label

Table 3-5: Manipulating Annotations (Continued)

Action	Microsoft Windows	Linux
Move annotation	Drag label	Drag label
Edit annotation	Click in text, then edit	Click in text, then edit
Delete annotation	**Shift** + select annotation, then press **Delete**	**Shift** + select annotation, then press **Delete**

Creating Subsystems

As your model increases in size and complexity, you can simplify it by grouping blocks into subsystems. Using subsystems has these advantages:

- It helps reduce the number of blocks displayed in your model window.
- It allows you to keep functionally related blocks together.
- It enables you to establish a hierarchical block diagram, where a Subsystem block is on one layer and the blocks that make up the subsystem are on another.

You can create a subsystem in two ways:

- Add a Subsystem block to your model, then open that block and add the blocks it contains to the subsystem window.
- Add the blocks that make up the subsystem, then group those blocks into a subsystem.

Creating a Subsystem by Adding the Subsystem Block

To create a subsystem before adding the blocks it contains, add a Subsystem block to the model, then add the blocks that make up the subsystem:

1 Copy the Subsystem block from the Signals & Systems library into your model.

2 Open the Subsystem block by double-clicking on it.

3 In the empty Subsystem window, create the subsystem. Use Inport blocks to represent input from outside the subsystem and Outport blocks to represent external output. For example, the subsystem below includes a Sum block and Inport and Outport blocks to represent input to and output from the subsystem.

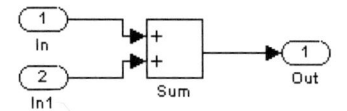

Creating a Subsystem by Grouping Existing Blocks

If your model already contains the blocks you want to convert to a subsystem, you can create the subsystem by grouping those blocks:

1 Enclose the blocks and connecting lines that you want to include in the subsystem within a bounding box. You cannot specify the blocks to be grouped by selecting them individually or by using the **Select All** command. For more information, see "Selecting Multiple Objects Using a Bounding Box" on page 3-7.

For example, this figure shows a model that represents a counter. The Sum and Unit Delay blocks are selected within a bounding box.

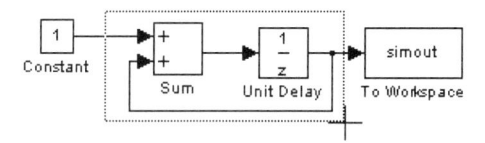

When you release the mouse button, the two blocks and all the connecting lines are selected.

2 Choose **Create Subsystem** from the **Edit** menu. Simulink replaces the selected blocks with a Subsystem block. This figure shows the model after choosing the **Create Subsystem** command (and resizing the Subsystem block so the port labels are readable).

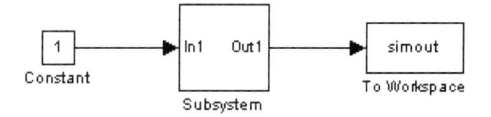

If you open the Subsystem block, Simulink displays the underlying system, as shown below. Notice that Simulink adds Inport and Outport blocks to represent input from and output to blocks outside the subsystem.

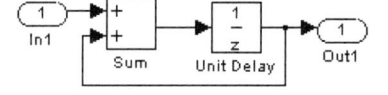

3-39

As with all blocks, you can change the name of the Subsystem block. Also, you can customize the icon and dialog box for the block using the masking feature, described in Chapter 6.

Labeling Subsystem Ports

Simulink labels ports on a Subsystem block. The labels are the names of Inport and Outport blocks that connect the subsystem to blocks outside the subsystem through these ports.

You can hide the port labels by selecting the Subsystem block, then choosing **Hide Port Labels** from the **Format** menu. You can also hide one or more port labels by selecting the appropriate Inport or Outport block in the subsystem and choosing **Hide Name** from the **Format** menu.

This figure shows two models. The subsystem on the left contains two Inport blocks and one Outport block. The Subsystem block on the right shows the labeled ports.

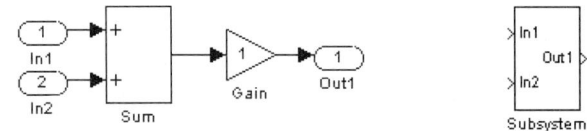

Subsystem with Inport and Outport blocks

Subsystem with labeled ports

Using Callback Routines

You can define MATLAB expressions that execute when the block diagram or a block is acted upon in a particular way. These expressions, called *callback routines*, are associated with block or model parameters. For example, the callback associated with a block's OpenFcn parameter is executed when the model user double-clicks on that block's name or path changes.

To define callback routines and associate them with parameters, use the set_param command (see set_param in the online documentation).

For example, this command evaluates the variable testvar when the user double-clicks on the Test block in mymodel.

    set_param('mymodel/Test', 'OpenFcn', testvar)

You can examine the clutch system (clutch.mdl) for routines associated with many model callbacks.

These tables list the parameters for which you can define callback routines, and indicate when those callback routines are executed. Routines that are executed before or after actions take place occur immediately before or after the action.

Table 3-6: Model Callback Parameters

Parameter	When Executed
CloseFcn	Before the block diagram is closed.
InitFcn	Called at start of model simulation.
PostLoadFcn	After the model is loaded. Defining a callback routine for this parameter might be useful for generating an interface that requires that the model has already been loaded.
PostSaveFcn	After the model is saved.
PreLoadFcn	Before the model is loaded. Defining a callback routine for this parameter might be useful for loading variables used by the model.
PreSaveFcn	Before the model is saved.
StartFcn	Before the simulation starts.
StopFcn	After the simulation stops. Output is written to workspace variables and files before the StopFcn is executed.

Table 3-7: Block Callback Parameters

Parameter	When Executed
CloseFcn	When the block is closed using the `close_system` command.
CopyFcn	After a block is copied. The callback is recursive for Subsystem blocks (that is, if you copy a Subsystem block that contains a block for which the CopyFcn parameter is defined, the routine is also executed). The routine is also executed if an `add_block` command is used to copy the block.
DeleteFcn	Before a block is deleted. This callback is recursive for Subsystem blocks.
DestroyFcn	When block has been destroyed.
InitFcn	Before the block diagram is compiled and before block parameters are evaluated.
LoadFcn	After the block diagram is loaded. This callback is recursive for Subsystem blocks.
ModelCloseFcn	Before the block diagram is closed. This callback is recursive for Subsystem blocks.
MoveFcn	When block is moved or resized.
NameChangeFcn	After a block's name and/or path changes. When a Subsystem block's path is changed, it recursively calls this function for all blocks it contains after calling its own NameChangeFcn routine.

Table 3-7: Block Callback Parameters (Continued)

Parameter	When Executed
OpenFcn	When the block is opened. This parameter is generally used with Subsystem blocks. The routine is executed when you double-click on the block or when an open_system command is called with the block as an argument. The OpenFcn parameter overrides the normal behavior associated with opening a block, which is to display the block's dialog box or to open the subsystem.
ParentCloseFcn	Before closing a subsystem containing the block or when the block is made part of a new subsystem using the new_system command (see new_system in the online documentation).
PreSaveFcn	Before the block diagram is saved. This callback is recursive for Subsystem blocks.
PostSaveFcn	After the block diagram is saved. This callback is recursive for Subsystem blocks.
StartFcn	After the block diagram is compiled and before the simulation starts.
StopFcn	At any termination of the simulation.
UndoDeleteFcn	When a block delete is undone.

Tips for Building Models

Here are some model-building hints you might find useful:

- Memory issues

  In general, the more memory, the better Simulink performs.

- Using hierarchy

  More complex models often benefit from adding the hierarchy of subsystems to the model. Grouping blocks simplifies the top level of the model and can make it easier to read and understand the model. For more information, see "Creating Subsystems" on page 3–38. The Model Browser (see "The Model Browser" on page 3-53) provides useful information about complex models.

- Cleaning up models

  Well organized and documented models are easier to read and understand. Signal labels and model annotations can help describe what is happening in a model. For more information, see "Signal Labels" on page 3–32 and "Annotations" on page 3–34.

- Modeling strategies

  If several of your models tend to use the same blocks, you might find it easier to save these blocks in a model. Then, when you build new models, just open this model and copy the commonly used blocks from it. You can create a block library by placing a collection of blocks into a system and saving the system. You can then access the system by typing its name in the MATLAB command window.

  Generally, when building a model, design it first on paper, then build it using the computer. Then, when you start putting the blocks together into a model, add the blocks to the model window before adding the lines that connect them. This way, you can reduce how often you need to open block libraries.

Modeling Equations

One of the most confusing issues for new Simulink users is how to model equations. Here are some examples that may improve your understanding of how to model equations.

Converting Celsius to Fahrenheit

To model the equation that converts Celsius temperature to Fahrenheit

$$T_F = \frac{9}{5}(T_C) + 32$$

First, consider the blocks needed to build the model:

- A Ramp block to input the temperature signal, from the Sources library
- A Constant block, to define a constant of 32, also from the Sources library
- A Gain block, to multiply the input signal by 9/5, from the Math library
- A Sum block, to add the two quantities, also from the Math library
- A Scope block to display the output, from the Sinks library

Next, gather the blocks into your model window.

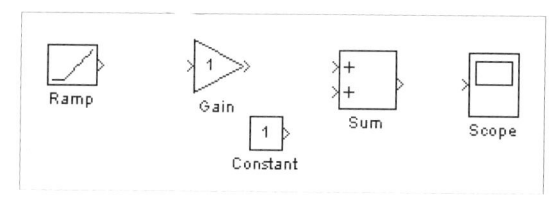

Assign parameter values to the Gain and Constant blocks by opening (double-clicking on) each block and entering the appropriate value. Then, click on the **Close** button to apply the value and close the dialog box.

Now, connect the blocks.

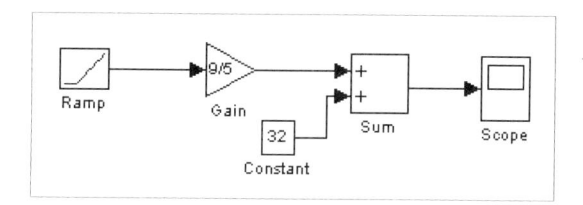

The Ramp block inputs Celsius temperature. Open that block and change the **Initial output** parameter to 0. The Gain block multiplies that temperature by the constant 9/5. The Sum block adds the value 32 to the result and outputs the Fahrenheit temperature.

Open the Scope block to view the output. Now, choose **Start** from the **Simulation** menu to run the simulation. The simulation will run for 10 seconds.

Modeling a Simple Continuous System

To model the differential equation

$$x'(t) = -2x(t) + u(t)$$

where $u(t)$ is a square wave with an amplitude of 1 and a frequency of 1 rad/sec. The Integrator block integrates its input, x', to produce x. Other blocks needed in this model include a Gain block and a Sum block. To generate a square wave, use a Signal Generator block and select the Square Wave form but change the default units to radians/sec. Again, view the output using a Scope block. Gather the blocks and define the gain.

In this model, to reverse the direction of the Gain block, select the block, then use the **Flip Block** command from the **Format** menu. Also, to create the branch line from the output of the Integrator block to the Gain block, hold down the **Ctrl** key while drawing the line. For more information, see "Drawing a Branch Line" on page 3–28. Now you can connect all the blocks.

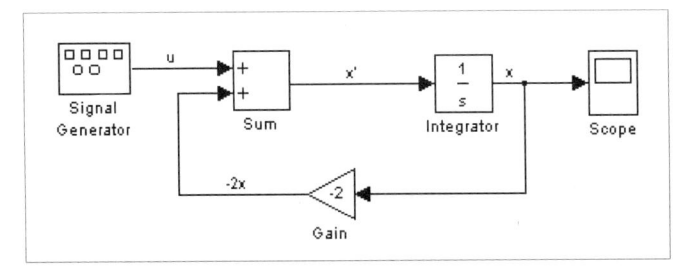

An important concept in this model is the loop that includes the Sum block, the Integrator block, and the Gain block. In this equation, x is the output of the Integrator block. It is also the input to the blocks that compute x', on which it is based. This relationship is implemented using a loop.

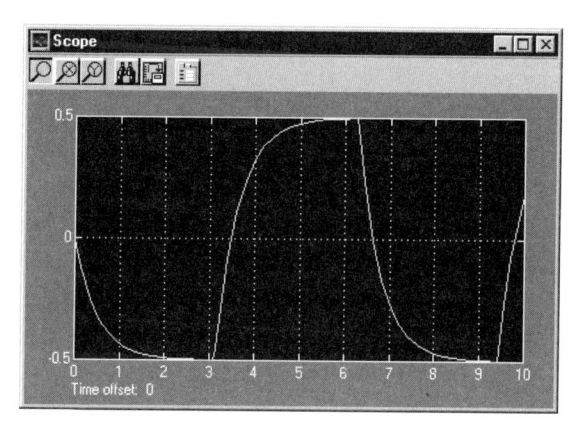

The Scope displays x at each time step. For a simulation lasting 10 seconds, the output looks like this.

The equation you modeled in this example can also be expressed as a transfer function. The model uses the Transfer Fcn block, which accepts u as input and outputs x. So, the block implements x/u. If you substitute sx for x' in the equation above,

$$sx = -2x + u$$

Solving for x gives

$$x = u/(s+2)$$

Or,

$$x/u = 1/(s+2)$$

The Transfer Fcn block uses parameters to specify the numerator and denominator coefficients. In this case, the numerator is 1 and the denominator is s+2. Specify both terms as vectors of coefficients of successively decreasing powers of s. In this case the numerator is [1] (or just 1) and the denominator is [1 2]. The model now becomes quite simple.

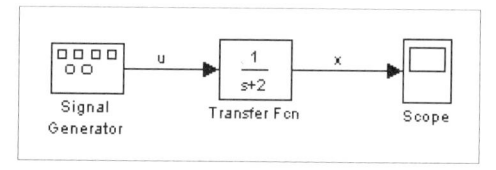

The results of this simulation are identical to those of the previous model.

3-47

Saving a Model

You can save a model by choosing either the **Save** or **Save As** command from the **File** menu. Simulink saves the model by generating a specially formatted file called the *model file* (with the .mdl extension) that contains the block diagram and block properties. The format of the model file is described in the online documentation.

If you are saving a model for the first time, use the **Save** command to provide a name and location to the model file. Model file names must start with a letter and can contain no more than 31 letters, numbers, and underscores.

If you are saving a model whose model file was previously saved, use the **Save** command to replace the file's contents or the **Save As** command to save the model with a new name or location.

Simulink follows this procedure while saving a model:

1 If the mdl file for the model already exists, it is renamed as a temporary file.

2 Simulink executes all block PreSaveFcn callback routines, then executes the block diagram's PreSaveFcn callback routine.

3 Simulink writes the model file to a new file using the same name and an extension of mdl.

4 Simulink executes all block PostSaveFcn callback routines, then executes the block diagram's PostSaveFcn callback routine.

5 Simulink deletes the temporary file.

If an error occurs during this process, Simulink renames the temporary file to the name of the original model file, writes the current version of the model to a file with an .err extension, and issues an error message. Simulink performs steps 2 through 4 even if an error occurs in an earlier step.

Printing a Block Diagram

You can print a block diagram by selecting **Print** from the **File** menu (on a Microsoft Windows system) or by using the `print` command in the MATLAB command window (on all platforms).

On a Microsoft Windows system, the **Print** menu item prints the block diagram in the current window.

Print Dialog Box

When you select the **Print** menu item, the **Print** dialog box appears. The **Print** dialog box enables you to selectively print systems within your model. Using the dialog box, you can:

- Print the current system only
- Print the current system and all systems above it in the model hierarchy
- Print the current system and all systems below it in the model hierarchy, with the option of looking into the contents of masked and library blocks
- Print all systems in the model, with the option of looking into the contents of masked and library blocks
- Print an overlay frame on each diagram

The portion of the **Print** dialog box that supports selective printing is similar on supported platforms. This figure shows how it looks on a Microsoft Windows system. In this figure, only the current system is to be printed.

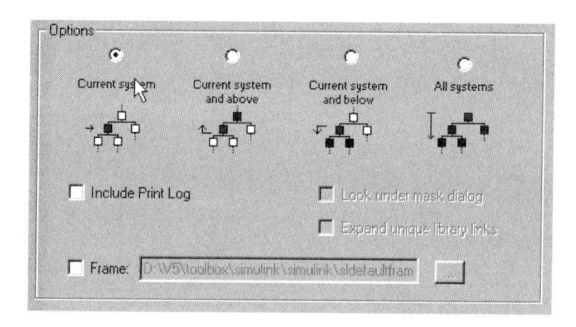

3-49

When you select either the **Current system and below** or **All systems** option, two check boxes become enabled. In this figure, **All systems** is selected.

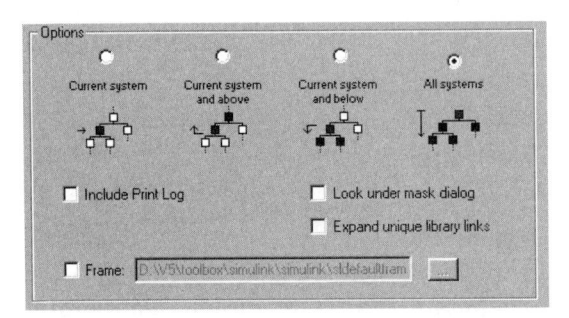

Selecting the **Look under mask dialog** check box prints the contents of masked subsystems when encountered at or below the level of the current block. When printing all systems, the top-level system is considered the current block so Simulink looks under any masked blocks encountered.

Selecting the **Expand unique library links** check box prints the contents of library blocks when those blocks are systems. Only one copy is printed regardless of how many copies of the block are contained in the model. For more information about libraries, see "Libraries" on page 3-21.

The print log lists the blocks and systems printed. To print the print log, select the **Include print log** check box.

Selecting the **Frame** check box prints a title block frame on each diagram. Enter the path to the title block frame in the adjacent edit box. You can create a customized title block frame, using MATLAB's frame editor. See `frameedit` in the online MATLAB reference for information on using the frame editor to create title block frames.

Print Command

The format of the `print` command is

```
print -ssys -device filename
```

`sys` is the name of the system to be printed. The system name must be preceded by the s switch identifier and is the only required argument. `sys` must be open or must have been open during the current session. If the system name contains spaces or takes more than one line, you need to specify the name as a string. See the examples below.

device specifies a device type. For a list and description of device types, see *Using MATLAB Graphics*.

filename is the PostScript file to which the output is saved. If *filename* exists, it is replaced. If *filename* does not include an extension, an appropriate one is appended.

For example, this command prints a system named untitled.

```
print -suntitled
```

This command prints the contents of a subsystem named Sub1 in the current system.

```
print -sSub1
```

This command prints the contents of a subsystem named Requisite Friction.

```
print (['-sRequisite Friction'])
```

The next example prints a system named Friction Model, a subsystem whose name appears on two lines. The first command assigns the newline character to a variable; the second prints the system.

```
cr = sprintf('\n');
print (['-sFriction' cr 'Model'])
```

Specifying Paper Size and Orientation

Simulink lets you specify the type and orientation of the paper used to print a model diagram. You can do this on all platforms by setting the model's PaperType and PaperOrientation properties, respectively (see the online documentation), using the set_param command. You can set the paper orientation alone, using MATLAB's orient command. On Windows, the **Print** dialog box lets you set the page type and orientation properties as well.

Positioning and Sizing a Diagram

You can use a model's PaperPositionMode and PaperPosition parameters to position and size the model's diagram on the printed page. The value of the PaperPosition parameter is a vector of form [left bottom width height]. The first two elements specify the bottom left corner of a rectangular area on the page, measured from the page's bottom left corner. The last two elements specify the width and height of the rectangle. When the model's

`PaperPositionMode` is manual, Simulink positions (and scales, if necessary) the model's diagram to fit inside the specified print rectangle. For example, the following commands

```
vdp
set_param('vdp', 'PaperType', 'usletter')
set_param('vdp', 'PaperOrientation', 'landscape')
set_param('vdp', 'PaperPositionMode', 'manual')
set_param('vdp', 'PaperPosition', [0.5 0.5 4 4])
print -svdp
```

print the block diagram of the `vdp` sample model in the lower left corner of a U.S. letter-size page in landscape orientation.

If `PaperPositionMode` is `auto`, Simulink centers the model diagram on the printed page, scaling the diagram, if necessary, to fit the page.

The Model Browser

The Model Browser enables you to:

- Navigate a model hierarchically
- Open systems in a model directly
- Determine the blocks contained in a model

The browser operates differently on Microsoft Windows and Linux platforms.

Using the Model Browser on Windows

To display the Model Browser pane, select **Model Browser** from the Simulink **View** menu. The model window splits into two panes. The left pane displays the browser, a tree-structured view of the block diagram displayed in the right pane.

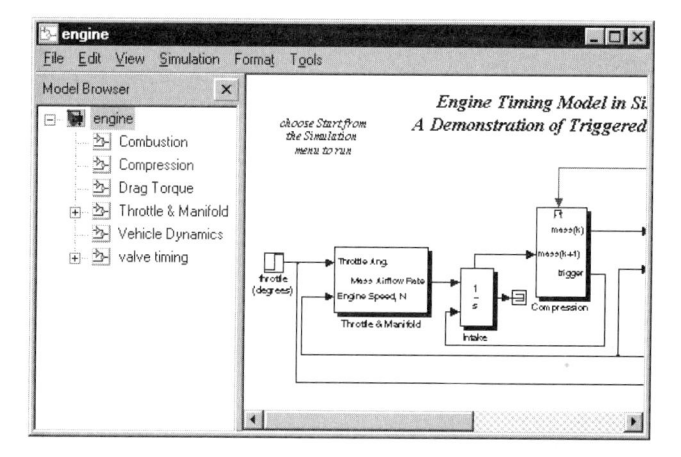

Each entry in the tree view corresponds to a subsystem in the model. You can expand/collapse the tree by clicking on the +/- boxes beside each subsystem, or by pressing the left/right arrow or +/- keys on your numeric keypad. You can move up/down the tree by pressing the up/down arrow on your keypad. Click on any subsystem to display its contents in the diagram view. To open a new window on a subsystem, double click the subsystem in the diagram view.

Using the Model Browser on Linux

To open the Model Browser, select **Show Browser** from the **File** menu. The Model Browser window appears, displaying information about the current model. This figure shows the Model Browser window displaying the contents of the `clutch` system.

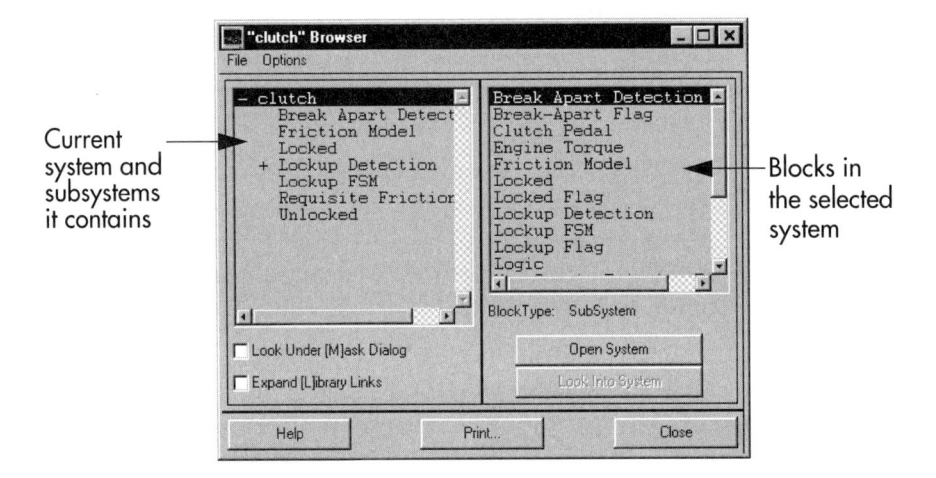

Current system and subsystems it contains → [systems list]

Blocks in the selected system ← [blocks list]

Contents of the Browser Window

The Model Browser window consists of:

- The systems list. The list on the left contains the current system and the subsystems it contains, with the current system selected.
- The blocks list. The list on the right contains the names of blocks in the selected system. Initially, this window displays blocks in the top-level system.
- The **File** menu, which contains the **Print**, **Close Model**, and **Close Browser** menu items.
- The **Options** menu, which contains these menu items: **Open System**, **Look Into System**, **Display Alphabetical/Hierarchical List**, **Expand All**, **Look Under Mask Dialog**, and **Expand Library Links**.
- **Options** check boxes and buttons: **Look Under [M]ask Dialog** and **Expand [L]ibrary Links** check boxes, and **Open System** and **Look Into System** buttons. By default, Simulink does not display contents of masked blocks and

blocks that are library links. These check boxes enable you to override the default.
- The block type of the selected block.
- Dialog box buttons: **Help**, **Print**, and **Close**.

Interpreting List Contents

Simulink identifies masked blocks, reference blocks, blocks with defined OpenFcn parameters, and systems that contain subsystems using these symbols before a block or system name:

- A plus sign (+) before a system name in the systems list indicates that the system is expandable, which means that it has systems beneath it. Double-click on the system name to expand the list and display its contents in the blocks list. When a system is expanded, a minus sign (–) appears before its name.
- [M] indicates that the block is masked, having either a mask dialog box or a mask workspace. For more information about masking, see Chapter 6.
- [L] indicates that the block is a reference block. For more information, see "Libraries" on page 3-21.
- [O] indicates that an open function (OpenFcn) callback is defined for the block. For more information about block callbacks, see "Using Callback Routines" on page 3-40.
- [S] indicates that the system is a Stateflow® block.

Opening a System

You can open any block or system whose name appears in the blocks list. To open a system:

1 In the systems list, select by single-clicking on the name of the parent system that contains the system you want to open. The parent system's contents appear in the blocks list.

2 Depending on whether the system is masked, linked to a library block, or has an open function callback, you open it as follows:

- If the system has no symbol to its left, double-click on its name or select its name and click on the **Open System** button.
- If the system has an [M] or [O] before its name, select the system name and click on the **Look Into System** button.

Looking into a Masked System or a Linked Block

By default, the Model Browser considers masked systems (identified by [M]) and linked blocks (identified by [L]) as blocks and not subsystems. If you click on **Open System** while a masked system or linked block is selected, the Model Browser displays the system or block's dialog box (**Open System** works the same way as double-clicking on the block in a block diagram). Similarly, if the block's OpenFcn callback parameter is defined, clicking on **Open System** while that block is selected executes the callback function.

You can direct the Model Browser to look beyond the dialog box or callback function by selecting the block in the blocks list, then clicking on **Look Into System**. The Model Browser displays the underlying system or block.

Displaying List Contents Alphabetically

By default, the systems list indicates the hierarchy of the model. Systems that contain systems are preceded with a plus sign (+). When those systems are expanded, the Model Browser displays a minus sign (–) before their names. To display systems alphabetically, select the **Display Alphabetical List** menu item on the **Options** menu.

Ending a Simulink Session

Terminate a Simulink session by closing all Simulink windows.

Terminate a MATLAB session by choosing one of these commands from the **File** menu:

- On a Microsoft Windows system: **Exit MATLAB**
- On a Linux system: **Quit MATLAB**

Running a Simulation

Introduction 4-2
Using Menu Commands 4-2
Running a Simulation from the Command Line 4-3

Running a Simulation Using Menu Commands 4-4
Setting Simulation Parameters and Choosing the Solver . . 4-4
Applying the Simulation Parameters 4-4
Starting the Simulation 4-4
Simulation Diagnostics Dialog Box 4-6

The Simulation Parameters Dialog Box 4-8
The Solver Page 4-8
The Workspace I/O Pane 4-17
The Diagnostics Pane 4-24

Improving Simulation Performance and Accuracy . . . 4-27
Speeding Up the Simulation 4-27
Improving Simulation Accuracy 4-28

Introduction

You can run a simulation either by using Simulink menu commands or by entering commands in the MATLAB command window.

Many users use menu commands while they develop and refine their models, then enter commands in the MATLAB command window to run the simulation in "batch" mode.

Using Menu Commands

Running a simulation using menu commands is easy and interactive. These commands let you select an ordinary differential equation (ODE) solver and define simulation parameters without having to remember command syntax. An important advantage is that you can perform certain operations interactively while a simulation is running:

- You can modify many simulation parameters, including the stop time, the solver, and the maximum step size.
- You can change the solver.
- You can simulate another system at the same time.
- You can click on a line to see the signal carried on that line on a floating (unconnected) Scope or Display block.
- You can modify the parameters of a block, as long as you do not cause a change in:
  - The number of states, inputs, or outputs
  - The sample time
  - The number of zero crossings
  - The vector length of any block parameters
  - The length of the internal block work vectors

You cannot make changes to the structure of the model, such as adding or deleting lines or blocks, during a simulation. If you need to make these kinds of changes, you need to stop the simulation, make the change, then start the simulation again to see the results of the change.

Running a Simulation from the Command Line

Running a simulation from the command line has these advantages over running a simulation using menu commands:

- You can simulate M-file and MEX-file models, as well as Simulink block diagram models.
- You can run a simulation from an M-file, allowing simulation and block parameters to be changed iteratively.

Running a Simulation Using Menu Commands

This section discusses how to use Simulink menu commands and the **Simulation Parameters** dialog box to run a simulation.

Setting Simulation Parameters and Choosing the Solver

You set the simulation parameters and select the solver by choosing **Parameters** from the **Simulation** menu. Simulink displays the **Simulation Parameters** dialog box, which uses three "pages" to manage simulation parameters:

- The **Solver** page allows you to set the start and stop times, choose the solver and specify solver parameters, and choose some output options.
- The **Workspace I/O** page manages input from and output to the MATLAB workspace.
- The **Diagnostics** page allows you to select the level of warning messages displayed during a simulation.

Each page of the dialog box, including the parameters you set on the page, is discussed in detail in "The Simulation Parameters Dialog Box" on page 4-8.

You can specify parameters as valid MATLAB expressions, consisting of constants, workspace variable names, MATLAB functions, and mathematical operators.

Applying the Simulation Parameters

After you have set the simulation parameters and selected the solver, you are ready to apply them to your model. Press the **Apply** button on the bottom of the dialog box to apply the parameters to the model. To apply the parameters and close the dialog box, press the **Close** button.

Starting the Simulation

After you have applied the solver and simulation parameters to your model, you are ready to run the simulation. Select **Start** from the **Simulation** menu to run the simulation. You can also use the keyboard shortcut, **Ctrl-T**. When you select **Start**, the menu item changes to **Stop**.

Your computer beeps to signal the completion of the simulation.

Note A common mistake that new Simulink users make is to start a simulation while the Simulink block library is the active window. Make sure your model window is the active window before starting a simulation.

To stop a simulation, choose **Stop** from the **Simulation** menu. The keyboard shortcut for stopping a simulation is **Ctrl-T**, the same as for starting a simulation.

You can suspend a running simulation by choosing **Pause** from the **Simulation** menu. When you select **Pause**, the menu item changes to **Continue**. You proceed with a suspended simulation by choosing **Continue**.

If the model includes any blocks that write output to a file or to the workspace, or if you select output options on the **Simulation Parameters** dialog box, Simulink writes the data when the simulation is terminated or suspended.

Simulation Diagnostics Dialog Box

If errors occur during a simulation, Simulink halts the simulation and displays the errors in the **Simulation Diagnostics** dialog box.

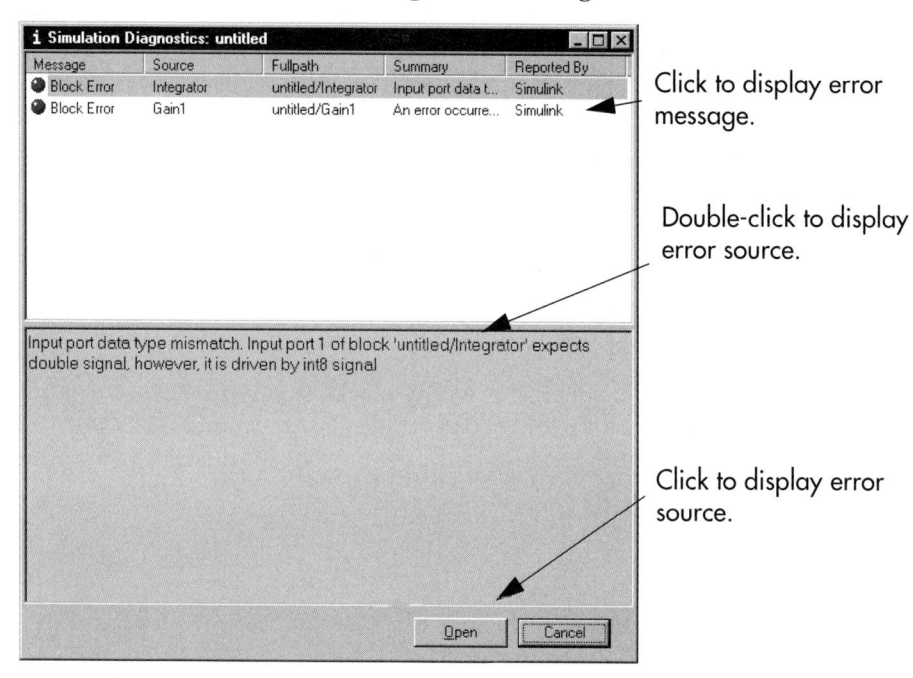

The dialog box has two panes. The upper pane consist of columns that display the following information for each error.

Message. Message type (for example, block error, warning, log)

Source. Name of the model element (for example, a block) that caused the error.

Fullpath. Path of the element that caused the error.

Summary. Error message abbreviated to fit in the column.

Reported By. Component that reported the error (for example, Simulink, Stateflow, Real-Time Workshop, etc.).

Running a Simulation Using Menu Commands

The lower pane initially contains the full content of the first error message listed in the top pane. You can display the content of other messages by single-clicking on their entries in the upper pane.

In addition to displaying the **Simulation Diagnostics** dialog box, Simulink also opens (if necessary) the diagram that contains the error source and highlights the source.

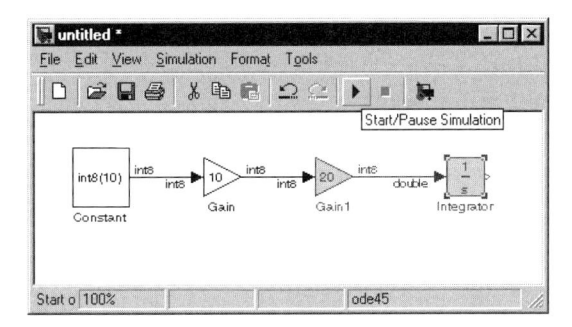

You can similarly display other error sources by double-clicking on the corresponding error message in the top pane, by double-clicking on the name of the error source in the error message (highlighted in blue), or by selecting the **Open** button on the dialog box.

4-7

The Simulation Parameters Dialog Box

This section discusses the simulation parameters, which you specify either on the **Simulation Parameters** dialog box or using the sim (see sim in the online documentation) and simset (see simset in the online documentation) commands. Parameters are described as they appear on the dialog box pages.

This table summarizes the actions performed by the dialog box buttons, which appear on the bottom of each dialog box page.

Table 4-1: Simulation Parameters Dialog Box Buttons

Button	Action
Ok	Applies the parameter values and closes the dialog box. During a simulation, the parameter values are applied immediately.
Cancel	Changes the parameter values back to the values they had when the dialog box was most recently opened and closes the dialog box.
Help	Displays help text for the dialog box page.
Apply	Applies the current parameter values and keeps the dialog box open. During a simulation, the parameter values are applied immediately.

The Solver Page

The **Solver** page appears when you first choose **Parameters** from the **Simulation** menu or when you select the **Solver** tab.

The **Solver** page allows you to:

- Set the simulation start and stop times
- Choose the solver and specify its parameters
- Select output options

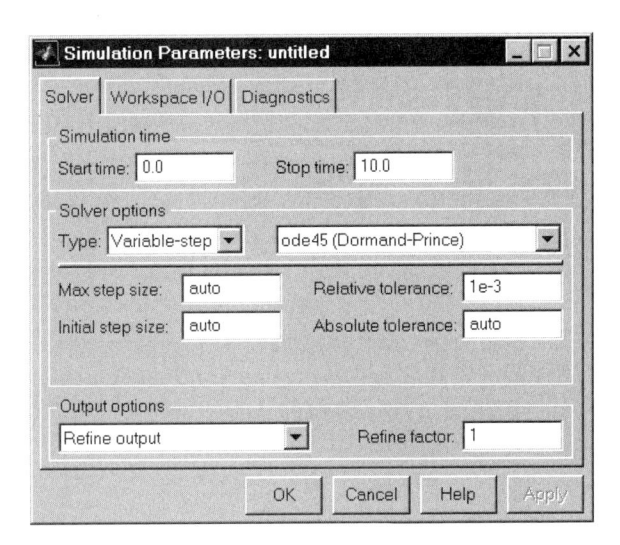

Simulation Time

You can change the start time and stop time for the simulation by entering new values in the **Start time** and **Stop time** fields. The default start time is 0.0 seconds and the default stop time is 10.0 seconds.

Simulation time and actual clock time are not the same. For example, running a simulation for 10 seconds will usually not take 10 seconds. The amount of time it takes to run a simulation depends on many factors, including the model's complexity, the solver's step sizes, and the computer's clock speed.

Solvers

Simulation of Simulink models involves the numerical integration of sets of ordinary differential equations (ODEs). Simulink provides a number of solvers for the simulation of such equations. Because of the diversity of dynamic system behavior, some solvers may be more efficient than others at solving a particular problem. To obtain accurate and fast results, take care when choosing the solver and setting parameters.

You can choose between variable-step and fixed-step solvers. *Variable-step solvers* can modify their step sizes during the simulation. They provide error control and zero crossing detection. *Fixed-step solvers* take the same step size during the simulation. They provide no error control and do not locate zero crossings. For a thorough discussion of solvers, see *Using MATLAB*.

Default Solvers. If you do not choose a solver, Simulink chooses one based on whether your model has states:

- If the model has continuous states, ode45 is used. ode45 is an excellent general purpose solver. However, if you know that your system is stiff and if ode45 is not providing acceptable results, try ode15s. For a definition of stiff, see the note at the end of the section "Variable-Step Solvers" on page 4-11.

- If the model has no continuous states, Simulink uses the variable-step solver called discrete and displays a message indicating that it is not using ode45. Simulink also provides a fixed-step solver called discrete. This model shows the difference between the two discrete solvers.

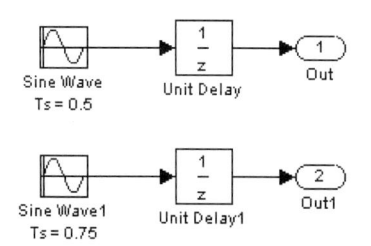

With sample times of 0.5 and 0.75, the *fundamental sample time* for the model is 0.25 seconds. The difference between the variable-step and the fixed-step discrete solvers is the time vector that each generates.

The fixed-step discrete solver generates this time vector.

```
[0.0 0.25 0.5 0.75 1.0 1.25 ...]
```

The variable-step discrete solver generates this time vector.

```
[0.0 0.5 0.75 1.0 1.5 2.0 2.25 ...]
```

The step size of the fixed-step discrete solver is the fundamental sample time. The variable-step discrete solver takes the largest possible steps.

Variable-Step Solvers. You can choose these variable-step solvers: `ode45`, `ode23`, `ode113`, `ode15s`, `ode23s`, and `discrete`. The default is `ode45` for systems with states, or `discrete` for systems with no states:

- `ode45` is based on an explicit Runge-Kutta (4,5) formula, the Dormand-Prince pair. It is a *one-step* solver; that is, in computing $y(t_n)$, it needs only the solution at the immediately preceding time point, $y(t_{n-1})$. In general, `ode45` is the best solver to apply as a "first try" for most problems.

- `ode23` is also based on an explicit Runge-Kutta (2,3) pair of Bogacki and Shampine. It may be more efficient than `ode45` at crude tolerances and in the presence of mild stiffness. `ode23` is a one-step solver.

- `ode113` is a variable order Adams-Bashforth-Moulton PECE solver. It may be more efficient than `ode45` at stringent tolerances. `ode113` is a *multistep* solver; that is, it normally needs the solutions at several preceding time points to compute the current solution.

- `ode15s` is a variable order solver based on the numerical differentiation formulas (NDFs). These are related to but are more efficient than the backward differentiation formulas, BDFs (also known as Gear's method). Like `ode113`, `ode15s` is a multistep method solver. If you suspect that a problem is stiff or if `ode45` failed or was very inefficient, try `ode15s`.

- `ode23s` is based on a modified Rosenbrock formula of order 2. Because it is a one-step solver, it may be more efficient than `ode15s` at crude tolerances. It can solve some kinds of stiff problems for which `ode15s` is not effective.

- `ode23t` is an implementation of the trapezoidal rule using a "free" interpolant. Use this solver if the problem is only moderately stiff and you need a solution without numerical damping.

- `ode23tb` is an implementation of TR-BDF2, an implicit Runge-Kutta formula with a first stage that is a trapezoidal rule step and a second stage that is a backward differentiation formula of order two. By construction, the same iteration matrix is used in evaluating both stages. Like `ode23s`, this solver may be more efficient than `ode15s` at crude tolerances.

- `discrete` (variable-step) is the solver Simulink chooses when it detects that your model has no continuous states.

> **Note** For a *stiff* problem, solutions can change on a time scale that is very short compared to the interval of integration, but the solution of interest changes on a much longer time scale. Methods not designed for stiff problems are ineffective on intervals where the solution changes slowly because they use time steps small enough to resolve the fastest possible change. Jacobian matrices are generated numerically for ode15s and ode23s. For more information, see Shampine, L. F., *Numerical Solution of Ordinary Differential Equations*, Chapman & Hall, 1994.

Fixed-Step Solvers. You can choose these fixed-step solvers: ode5, ode4, ode3, ode2, ode1, and `discrete`:

- ode5 is the fixed-step version of ode45, the Dormand-Prince formula.
- ode4 is RK4, the fourth-order Runge-Kutta formula.
- ode3 is the fixed-step version of ode23, the Bogacki-Shampine formula.
- ode2 is Heun's method, also known as the improved Euler formula.
- ode1 is Euler's method.
- `discrete` (fixed-step) is a fixed-step solver that performs no integration. It is suitable for models having no states and for which zero crossing detection and error control are not important.

If you think your simulation may be providing unsatisfactory results, see "Improving Simulation Performance and Accuracy" on page 4-27.

Solver Options

The default solver parameters provide accurate and efficient results for most problems. In some cases, however, tuning the parameters can improve performance. (For more information about tuning these parameters, see "Improving Simulation Performance and Accuracy" on page 4-27). You can tune the selected solver by changing parameter values on the **Solver** panel.

Step Sizes

For variable-step solvers, you can set the maximum and suggested initial step size parameters. By default, these parameters are automatically determined, indicated by the value `auto`.

For fixed-step solvers, you can set the fixed step size. The default is also `auto`.

Maximum Step Size. The **Max step size** parameter controls the largest time step the solver can take. The default is determined from the start and stop times.

$$h_{max} = \frac{t_{stop} - t_{start}}{50}$$

Generally, the default maximum step size is sufficient. If you are concerned about the solver missing significant behavior, change the parameter to prevent the solver from taking too large a step. If the time span of the simulation is very long, the default step size may be too large for the solver to find the solution. Also, if your model contains periodic or nearly periodic behavior and you know the period, set the maximum step size to some fraction (such as 1/4) of that period.

In general, for more output points, change the refine factor, not the maximum step size. For more information, see "Refine Output" on page 4-16.

Initial step size. By default, the solvers select an initial step size by examining the derivatives of the states at the start time. If the first step size is too large, the solver may step over important behavior. The initial step size parameter is a *suggested* first step size. The solver tries this step size but reduces it if error criteria are not satisfied.

Error Tolerances

The solvers use standard local error control techniques to monitor the error at each time step. During each time step, the solvers compute the state values at the end of the step and also determine the *local error*, the estimated error of these state values. They then compare the local error to the *acceptable error*, which is a function of the relative tolerance (*rtol*) and absolute tolerance (*atol*). If the error is greater than the acceptable error for *any* state, the solver reduces the step size and tries again:

- *Relative tolerance* measures the error relative to the size of each state. The relative tolerance represents a percentage of the state's value. The default, 1e-3, means that the computed state will be accurate to within 0.1%.
- *Absolute tolerance* is a threshold error value. This tolerance represents the acceptable error as the value of the measured state approaches zero.

The error for the ith state, e_i, is required to satisfy

$$e_i \leq max(rtol \times |x_i|, atol_i)$$

The figure below shows a plot of a state and the regions in which the acceptable error is determined by the relative tolerance and the absolute tolerance.

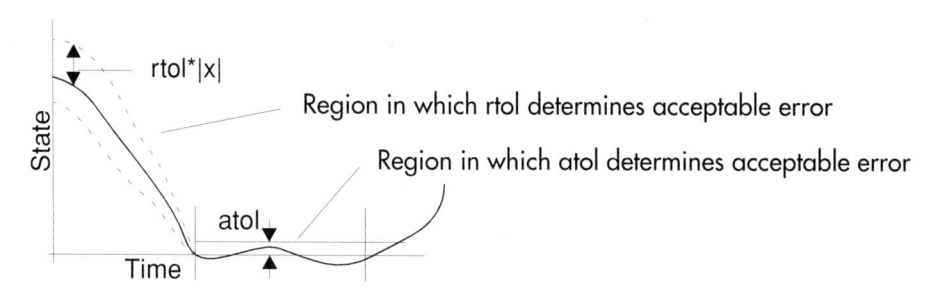

If you specify auto (the default), Simulink sets the absolute tolerance for each state initially to 1e-6. As the simulation progresses, Simulink resets the absolute tolerance for each state to the maximum value that the state has assumed thus far times the relative tolerance for that state. Thus, if a state goes from 0 to 1 and reltol is 1e-3, then by the end of the simulation the abstol is set to 1e-3 also. If a state goes from 0 to 1000, then the abstol is set to 1.

If the computed setting is not suitable, you can determine an appropriate setting yourself. You might have to run a simulation more than once to determine an appropriate value for the absolute tolerance. If the magnitudes of the states vary widely, it might be appropriate to specify different absolute tolerance values for different states. You can do this on the Integrator block's dialog box.

The Maximum Order for ode15s

The ode15s solver is based on NDF formulas of order one through five. Although the higher order formulas are more accurate, they are less stable. If your model is stiff and requires more stability, reduce the maximum order to 2 (the highest order for which the NDF formula is A-stable). When you choose the ode15s solver, the dialog box displays this parameter.

As an alternative, you might try using the ode23s solver, which is a fixed-step, lower order (and A-stable) solver.

Multitasking Options

If you select a fixed-step solver, the **Solver** page of the **Simulation Parameters** dialog box displays a **Mode** options list. The list allows you to select one of the following simulation modes.

MultiTasking. This mode issues an error if it detects an illegal sample rate transition between blocks, that is, a direct connection between blocks operating at different sample rates. In real-time multitasking systems, illegal sample rate transitions between tasks can result in a task's output not being available when needed by another task. By checking for such transitions, multitasking mode helps you to create valid models of real-world multitasking systems, where sections of your model represent concurrent tasks.

Use *rate transition* blocks to eliminate illegal rate transitions from your model. Simulink provides two such blocks: Unit Delay (see `Unit Delay` in the online documentation) and Zero-Order Hold (see `Zero-Order Hold` in the online documentation). To eliminate an illegal slow-to-fast transition, insert a Unit Delay block running at the slow rate between the slow output port and the fast input port. To eliminate an illegal fast-to-slow transition, insert a Zero-Order Hold block running at the slow rate between the fast output port and the slow input port. For more information, see Chapter 7, "Models with Multiple Sample Rates," in the *Real-Time Workshop Users Guide*.

SingleTasking. This mode does not check for sample rate transitions among blocks. This mode is useful when you are modeling a single-tasking system. In such systems, task synchronization is not an issue.

Auto. This option causes Simulink to use single-tasking mode if all blocks operate at the same rate and multitasking mode if the model contains blocks operating at different rates.

Output Options

The **Output options** area of the dialog box enables you to control how much output the simulation generates. You can choose from three pop-up options:

- Refine output
- Produce additional output
- Produce specified output only

Refine Output. The **Refine output** choice provides additional output points when the simulation output is too coarse. This parameter provides an integer number of output points between time steps; for example, a refine factor of 2 provides output midway between the time steps, as well as at the steps. The default refine factor is 1.

To get smoother output, it is much faster to change the refine factor instead of reducing the step size. When the refine factor is changed, the solvers generate additional points by evaluating a continuous extension formula at those points. Changing the refine factor does not change the steps used by the solver.

The refine factor applies to variable-step solvers and is most useful when using `ode45`. The `ode45` solver is capable of taking large steps; when graphing simulation output, you may find that output from this solver is not sufficiently smooth. If this is the case, run the simulation again with a larger refine factor. A value of 4 should provide much smoother results.

Produce Additional Output. The **Produce additional output** choice enables you to specify directly those additional times at which the solver generates output. When you select this option, Simulink displays an **Output Times** field on the **Solver** page. Enter a MATLAB expression in this field that evaluates to an additional time or a vector of additional times. The additional output is produced using a continuous extension formula at the additional times. Unlike the refine factor, this option changes the simulation step size so that time steps coincide with the times that you have specified for additional output.

Produce Specified Output Only. The **Produce specified output only** choice provides simulation output *only* at the specified output times. This option changes the simulation step size so that time steps coincide with the times that you have specified for producing output. This choice is useful when comparing different simulations to ensure that the simulations produce output at the same times.

Comparing Output Options. A sample simulation generates output at these times.

```
0, 2.5, 5, 8.5, 10
```

Choosing **Refine output** and specifying a refine factor of 2 generates output at these times.

```
0, 1.25, 2.5, 3.75, 5, 6.75, 8.5, 9.25, 10
```

Choosing the **Produce additional output** option and specifying [0:10] generates output at these times.

    0, 1, 2, 3, 4, 5, 6, 7, 8, 9, 10

and perhaps at additional times, depending on the step-size chosen by the variable-step solver.

Choosing the **Produce Specified Output Only** option and specifying [0:10] generates output at these times.

    0, 1, 2, 3, 4, 5, 6, 7, 8, 9, 10

The Workspace I/O Page

You can direct simulation output to workspace variables and get input and initial states from the workspace. On the **Simulation Parameters** dialog box, select the **Workspace I/O** tab. This dialog box appears.

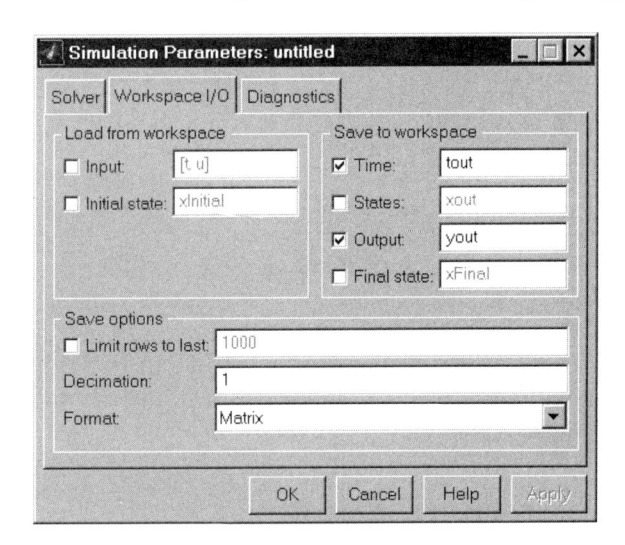

Loading Input from the Base Workspace

Simulink can apply input from a model's base workspace to the model's top-level inports during a simulation run. To specify this option, check the **Input** box in the **Load from workspace** area of the **Workspace I/O** page. Then, enter an external input specification (see below) in the adjacent edit box and select **Apply**.

4-17

The external input can take any of the following forms.

External Input Matrix. The first column of an external input matrix must be a vector of times in ascending order. The remaining columns specify input values. In particular, each column represents the input for a different Inport block signal (in sequential order) and each row is the input value for the corresponding time point. Simulink linearly interpolates or extrapolates input values as necessary, if the **Interpolate data** option is selected for the corresponding inport (see "Interpolate data" in the online documentation).

The total number of columns of the input matrix must equal n + 1, where n is the total number of signals entering the model's inports. If you define t and u in the base workspace, you do not need to enter an external input specification for the model. This is because the default external input specification for a model is [t,u].

For example, suppose that a model has two inports, one of which accepts two signals and the other, one signal. Also, suppose that the base workspace defines u and t as follows.

```
t = (0:0.1:1)';
u = [sin(t), cos(t), 4*cos(t)];
```

Then, to specify the external input for this model, simply check the model's external input box.

Structure with Time. Simulink can read data from the workspace in the form of a structure whose name is specified in the **Input** text field. The input structure must have two top-level fields: `time` and `signals`. The `time` field contains a column vector of the simulation times. The `signals` field contains an array of substructures, each of which corresponds to a model input port. Each substructure has the field: `values`. The `values` field contains a column vector of inputs for the corresponding input port.

For example, consider the following model, which has two inputs.

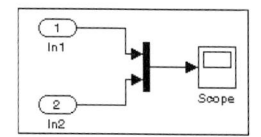

Suppose that the base workspace defines a model input vector, a, as follows.

```
a.time = (0:0.1:1)';
a.signals(1).values = sin(a.time);
a.signals(2).values = cos(a.time);
```

Then, to specify a as the external input for this model, check the **Input** box and enter a in the adjacent text field.

Note Simulink can read back simulation data saved to the workspace in the **Structure with time** output format. See "Structure with Time" on page 4-21 for more information.

Structure. The structure format is the same as the **Structure with time** format except that time field is empty. For example, in the preceding example, you could set the time field as follows.

```
a.time = [ ]
```

In this case, Simulink reads the input for the first time step from the first element of an inport's value array, the value for the second time step from the second element of the value array, etc.

Note Simulink can read back simulation data saved to the workspace in the **Structure** output format. See "Structure" on page 4-21 for more information.

Per-Port Structures. This format consists of a separate structure-with-time or structure-without-time for each port. Each port's input data structure has only one signals field. To specify this option, enter the names of the structures in the **Input** text field as a comma-separated list in1, in2, ..., inN, where in1 is the data for your model's first port, in2 for the second inport, and so on.

External Input Time Expression. The time expression can be any MATLAB expression that evaluates to a row vector equal in length to the number of signals entering the model's inports. For example, suppose that a model has one vector inport that accepts two signals. Furthermore, suppose that timefcn is a user-defined function that returns a row vector two elements long. The following are valid input time expressions for such a model.

`'[3*sin(t), cos(2*t)]'`

`'4*timefcn(w*t)+7'`

Simulink evaluates the expression at each step of the simulation, applying the resulting values to the model's inports. Note that Simulink defines the variable t when it runs the simulation. Also, you can omit the time variable in expressions for functions of one variable. For example, Simulink interprets the expression `sin` as `sin(t)`.

Saving Output to the Workspace

You can specify return variables by selecting the **Time**, **States**, and/or **Output** check boxes in the **Save to workspace** area of this dialog box page. Specifying return variables causes Simulink to write values for the time, state, and output trajectories (as many as are selected) into the workspace.

To assign values to different variables, specify those variable names in the field to the right of the check boxes. To write output to more than one variable, specify the variable names in a comma-separated list. Simulink saves the simulation times in a vector have the name specified in the **Save to Workspace** area.

Note Simulink saves the output to the workspace at the base sample rate of the model. Use a To Workspace block if you want to save output at a different sample rate (see `To Workspace` in the online documentation).

The **Save options** area enables you to specify the format and restrict the amount of output saved.

Format options for model states and outputs are:

Matrix. Simulink saves the model states in a matrix that has the name specified in the **Save to Workspace** area (for example, `xout`). Each column of the state matrix corresponds to a model state, each row to the states at a specific time. The model output matrix has the name specified in the **Save to**

Workspace area (for example, yout). Each column corresponds to a model outport, each row to the outputs at a specific time.

Structure with Time. Simulink saves the model's outputs in a structure having the name specified in the **Save to Workspace** area (for example, yout). The structure has two top-level fields: time and signals. The time field contains a vector of the simulation times. The signals field contains an array of substructures, each of which corresponds to a model outport. Each substructure has three fields: values, label, blockName. The values field contains a vector of outputs for the corresponding outport. The label field specifies the label of the signal connected to the outport. The blockName field specifies the name of the outport. Simulink saves the model's states in a structure have the same organization as the model output structure.

Structure. This format is the same as the preceding except that Simulink does not store simulation times in the time field of the saved structure.

Per-Port Structures. This format consists of a separate structure-with-time or structure-without-time for each output port. Each output data structure has only one signals field. To specify this option, enter the names of the structures in the **Output** text field as a comma-separated list out1, out2, ..., outN, where out1 is the data for your model's first port, out2 for the second inport, and so on.

To set a limit on the number of rows of data saved, select the check box labeled **Limit rows to last** and specify the number of rows to save. To apply a decimation factor, enter a value in the field to the right of the **Decimation** label. For example, a value of 2 saves every other point generated.

Loading and Saving States

Initial conditions, which are applied to the system at the start of the simulation, are generally set in the blocks. You can override initial conditions set in the blocks by specifying them in the **States** area of this page.

You can also save the final states for a simulation and apply them to another simulation. This feature might be useful when you want to save a steady-state solution and restart the simulation at that known state. The states are saved in the format that you select in the Save options area of the Workspace I/O page. If you select Structure or Structure with Time, the saved format is as follows:

Structure with Time. Simulink saves the model's states in a structure having the name specified in the **Final State** field of the **Save to Workspace** area (for example, xFinal). The structure has two top-level fields: time and signals. The time field contains a vector of the simulation times. The signals field contains an array of substructures, each of which corresponds to a block that has states. Each substructure has three fields: values, label, blockName. The values field contains a vector of states for the corresponding block. The label field can be either CState (for continuous state) or DState_n where n can be 1, 2, 3 ... to the maximum number of sets of discrete states for the corresponding block. The blockName field specifies the name of the block represented by this structure element.

Structure. This format is the same as the preceding except that Simulink does not store simulation times in the time field of the saved structure

You load states by selecting the **Initial State** check box and specifying the name of a variable that contains the initial state values. This variable can be a matrix or a structure of the same form as is used to save final states. This allows Simulink to set the initial states for the current session to the final states saved in previous session, using the **Structure** or **Structure with time** format.

If the check box is not selected or the state vector is empty ([ ]), Simulink uses the initial conditions defined in the blocks.

You save the final states (the values of the states at the termination of the simulation) by selecting the **Final State** check box and entering a variable in the adjacent edit field.

When the Model Has Multiple States. If you want to specify the initial conditions for a model that has multiple states, you need to determine the order of the states. You can determine a model's initial conditions and the ordering of its states with this command

    [sizes, x0, xstord] = sys([], [], [], 0)

where sys is the model name. The command returns:

- sizes, a vector that indicates certain model characteristics. Only the first two elements apply to initial conditions: sizes(1) is the number of continuous states, and sizes(2) is the number of discrete states. The sizes vector is described in more detail in the companion volume to this guide, *Writing S-Functions*, which is accessible from the Help Desk.

- x0, the block initial conditions.
- xstord, a string matrix that contains the full path name of all blocks in the model that have states. The order of the blocks in the xstord and x0 vectors are the same.

For example, this statement obtains the values of the initial conditions and the ordering of the states for the vdp model (the example shows only the values for sizes(1), the number of continuous states, and sizes(2), the number of discrete states).

```
[sizes, x0, xstord] = vdp([], [], [], 0)

sizes =
    2
    0

x0 =
    2
    0

xstord =
    'vdp/Integrator1'
    'vdp/Integrator2'
```

The Diagnostics Page

You can indicate the desired action for many types of events or conditions that can be encountered during a simulation by selecting the **Diagnostics** tab on the **Simulation Parameters** dialog box. This dialog box appears.

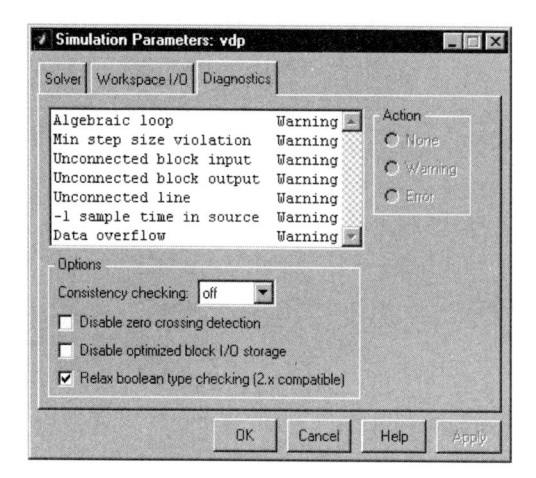

For each event type, you can choose whether you want no message, a warning message, or an error message. A warning message does not terminate a simulation, but an error message does.

Consistency Checking

Consistency checking is a debugging tool that validates certain assumptions made by Simulink's ODE solvers. Its main use is to make sure that S-functions adhere to the same rules as Simulink built-in blocks. Because consistency checking results in a significant decrease in performance (up to 40%), it should generally be set to off. Use consistency checking to validate your S-functions and to help you determine the cause of unexpected simulation results.

To perform efficient integration, Simulink saves (caches) certain values from one time step for use in the next time step. For example, the derivatives at the end of a time step can generally be reused at the start of the next time step. The solvers take advantage of this to avoid redundant derivative calculations.

Another purpose of consistency checking is to ensure that blocks produce constant output when called with a given value of t (time). This is important for the stiff solvers (ode23s and ode15s) because, while calculating the

Jacobian, the block's output functions may be called many times at the same value of t.

When consistency checking is enabled, Simulink recomputes the appropriate values and compares them to the cached values. If the values are not the same, a consistency error occurs. Simulink compares computed values for these quantities:

- Outputs
- Zero crossings
- Derivatives
- States

Disabling Zero Crossing Detection

You can disable zero crossing detection for a simulation. For a model that has zero crossings, disabling the detection of zero crossings may speed up the simulation but might have an adverse effect on the accuracy of simulation results.

This option disables zero crossing detection for those blocks that have intrinsic zero crossing detection. It does not disable zero crossing detection for the Hit Crossing block.

Disable Optimized I/O Storage

Checking this option causes Simulink to allocate a separate memory buffer for each block's I/O values instead of reusing memory buffers. This can substantially increase the amount of memory required to simulate large models. So you should select this option only when you need to debug a model. In particular, you should disable buffer reuse if you need to:

- Debug a C-MEX s-function
- Use a floating scope or display to inspect signals in a model that you are debugging

  Simulink opens an error dialog if buffer reuse is enabled and you attempt to use a floating scope or display to display a signal whose buffer has been reused.

Relax Boolean Type Checking (2.x Compatible)

Checking this option causes blocks that would otherwise require inputs of type `boolean` to accept inputs of type `double`. This ensures compatibility with models created by versions of Simulink earlier than Simulink 3. For example, consider the following model.

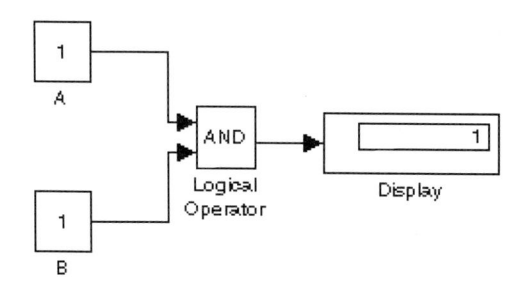

This model connects signals of type `double` to a Logical Operator block that ordinarily requires inputs of type `boolean`. Consequently, this model runs without error only if the **Relax boolean type checking** option is selected.

Improving Simulation Performance and Accuracy

Simulation performance and accuracy can be affected by many things, including the model design and choice of simulation parameters.

The solvers handle most model simulations accurately and efficiently with their default parameter values. However, some models will yield better results if you adjust solver and simulation parameters. Also, if you know information about your model's behavior, your simulation results can be improved if you provide this information to the solver.

Speeding Up the Simulation

Slow simulation speed can have many causes. Here are a few:

- Your model includes a MATLAB Fcn block. When a model includes a MATLAB Fcn block, the MATLAB interpreter is called at each time step, drastically slowing down the simulation. Use the built-in Fcn block or Elementary Math block whenever possible.
- Your model includes an M-file S-function. M-file S-functions also cause the MATLAB interpreter to be called at each time step. Consider either converting the S-function to a subsystem or to a C-MEX file S-function.
- Your model includes a Memory block. Using a Memory block causes the variable-order solvers (`ode15s` and `ode113`) to be reset back to order 1 at each time step.
- The maximum step size is too small. If you changed the maximum step size, try running the simulation again with the default value (`auto`).
- Did you ask for too much accuracy? The default relative tolerance (0.1% accuracy) is usually sufficient. For models with states that go to zero, if the absolute tolerance parameter is too small, the simulation may take too many steps around the near-zero state values. See the discussion of error in "Error Tolerances" on page 4-13.
- The time scale may be too long. Reduce the time interval.
- The problem may be stiff but you're using a nonstiff solver. Try using `ode15s`.
- The model uses sample times that are not multiples of each other. Mixing sample times that are not multiples of each other causes the solver to take small enough steps to ensure sample time hits for all sample times.

- The model contains an algebraic loop. The solutions to algebraic loops are iteratively computed at every time step. Therefore, they severely degrade performance. For more information, see "Algebraic Loops" on page 7-7.
- Your model feeds a Random Number block into an Integrator block. For continuous systems, use the Band-Limited White Noise block in the Sources library.

Improving Simulation Accuracy

To check your simulation accuracy, run the simulation over a reasonable time span. Then, reduce either the relative tolerance to 1e-4 (the default is 1e-3) or the absolute tolerance and run it again. Compare the results of both simulations. If the results are not significantly different, you can feel confident that the solution has converged.

If the simulation misses significant behavior at its start, reduce the initial step size to ensure that the simulation does not "step over" the significant behavior.

If the simulation results become unstable over time:

- Your system may be unstable.
- If you are using ode15s, you may need to restrict the maximum order to 2 (the maximum order for which the solver is A-stable) or try using the ode23s solver.

If the simulation results do not appear to be accurate:

- For a model that has states whose values approach zero, if the absolute tolerance parameter is too large, the simulation will take too few steps around areas of near-zero state values. Reduce this parameter value or adjust it for individual states in the Integrator dialog box.
- If reducing the absolute tolerances do not sufficiently improve the accuracy, reduce the size of the relative tolerance parameter to reduce the acceptable error and force smaller step sizes and more steps.

Analyzing Simulation Results

Viewing Output Trajectories 5-2
Using the Scope Block 5-2
Using Return Variables 5-2
Using the To Workspace Block 5-3

Linearization 5-4

Equilibrium Point Determination 5-7

Viewing Output Trajectories

Output trajectories from Simulink can be plotted using one of three methods:

- Feeding a signal into either a Scope or an XY Graph block
- Writing output to return variables and using MATLAB plotting commands
- Writing output to the workspace using To Workspace blocks and plotting the results using MATLAB plotting commands

Using the Scope Block

You can use display output trajectories on a Scope block during a simulation. This simple model shows an example of the use of the Scope block.

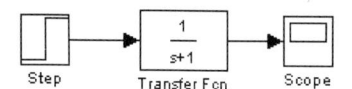

The display on the Scope shows the output trajectory. The Scope block enables you to zoom in on an area of interest or save the data to the workspace.

The XY Graph block enables you to plot one signal against another.

These blocks are described in the online documentation.

Using Return Variables

By returning time and output histories, you can use MATLAB plotting commands to display and annotate the output trajectories.

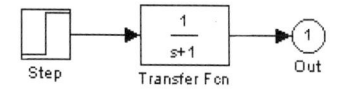

The block labeled Out is an Outport block from the Signals & Systems library. The output trajectory, yout, is returned by the integration solver. For more information, see the online documentation.

You can also run this simulation from the **Simulation** menu by specifying variables for the time, output, and states on the **Workspace I/O** page of the **Simulation Parameters** dialog box. You can then plot these results using

```
plot(tout,yout)
```

Using the To Workspace Block

The To Workspace block can be used to return output trajectories to the MATLAB workspace. The model below illustrates this use.

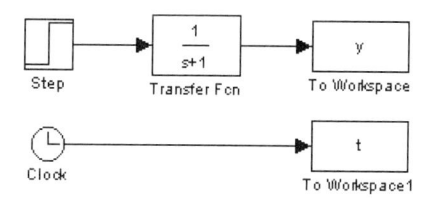

The variables y and t appear in the workspace when the simulation is complete. The time vector is stored by feeding a Clock block into a To Workspace block. The time vector can also be acquired by entering a variable name for the time on the **Workspace I/O** page of the **Simulation Parameters** dialog box for menu-driven simulations, or by returning it using the `sim` command (see the online documentation for more information).

The To Workspace block can accept a vector input, with each input element's trajectory stored as a column vector in the resulting workspace variable.

Linearization

Simulink provides the `linmod` and `dlinmod` functions to extract linear models in the form of the state-space matrices A, B, C, and D. State-space matrices describe the linear input-output relationship as

$$\dot{x} = Ax + Bu$$
$$y = Cx + Du$$

where x, u, and y are state, input, and output vectors, respectively. For example, the following model is called `lmod`.

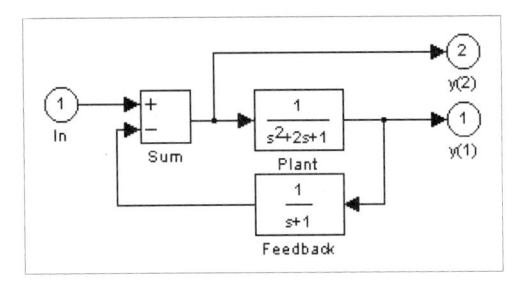

To extract the linear model of this Simulink system, enter this command.

```
[A,B,C,D] = linmod('lmod')
A =
    -2    -1    -1
     1     0     0
     0     1    -1
B =
     1
     0
     0
C =
     0     1     0
     0     0    -1
D =
     0
     1
```

Inputs and outputs must be defined using Inport and Outport blocks from the Signals & Systems library. Source and sink blocks do not act as inputs and outputs. Inport blocks can be used in conjunction with source blocks using a Sum block. Once the data is in the state-space form or converted to an LTI object, you can apply functions in the Control System Toolbox for further analysis:

- Conversion to an LTI object
  ```
  sys = ss(A,B,C,D);
  ```
- Bode phase and magnitude frequency plot
  ```
  bode(A,B,C,D) or bode(sys)
  ```
- Linearized time response
  ```
  step(A,B,C,D) or step(sys)
  impulse(A,B,C,D) or impulse(sys)
  lsim(A,B,C,D,u,t) or lsim(sys,u,t)
  ```

Other functions in the Control System Toolbox and Robust Control Toolbox can be used for linear control system design.

When the model is nonlinear, an operating point may be chosen at which to extract the linearized model. The nonlinear model is also sensitive to the perturbation sizes at which the model is extracted. These must be selected to balance the trade-off between truncation and roundoff error. Extra arguments to linmod specify the operating point and perturbation points.

```
[A,B,C,D] = linmod('sys', x, u, pert, xpert, upert)
```

For discrete systems or mixed continuous and discrete systems, use the function dlinmod for linearization. This has the same calling syntax as linmod except that the second right-hand argument must contain a sample time at which to perform the linearization. For more information, see linfun in the online documentation.

Using linmod to linearize a model that contains Derivative or Transport Delay blocks can be troublesome. Before linearizing, replace these blocks with specially designed blocks that avoid the problems. These blocks are in the Simulink Extras library in the Linearization sublibrary. You access the Extras library by opening the Blocksets & Toolboxes icon.

- For the Derivative block, use the Switched derivative for linearization.
- For the Transport Delay block, use the Switched transport delay for linearization. (Using this block requires that you have the Control System Toolbox.)

When using a Derivative block, you can also try to incorporate the derivative term in other blocks. For example, if you have a Derivative block in series with a Transfer Fcn block, it is better implemented (although this is not always possible) with a single Transfer Fcn block of the form

$$\frac{s}{s+a}$$

In this example, the blocks on the left of this figure can be replaced by the block on the right.

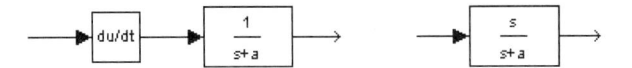

Equilibrium Point Determination

The Simulink `trim` function determines steady-state equilibrium points. Consider, for example, this model, called `lmod`.

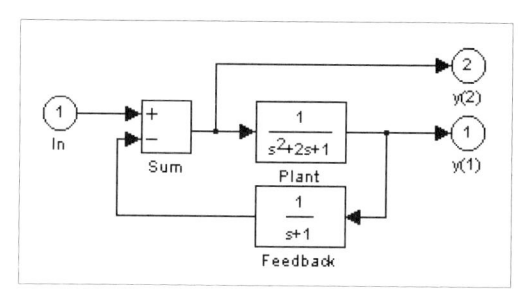

You can use the `trim` function to find the values of the input and the states that set both outputs to 1. First, make initial guesses for the state variables (x) and input values (u), then set the desired value for the output (y).

```
x = [0; 0; 0];
u = 0;
y = [1; 1];
```

Use index variables to indicate which variables are fixed and which can vary.

```
ix = [];      % Don't fix any of the states
iu = [];      % Don't fix the input
iy = [1;2];   % Fix both output 1 and output 2
```

5 Analyzing Simulation Results

Invoking `trim` returns the solution. Your results may differ due to roundoff error.

```
[x,u,y,dx] = trim('lmod',x,u,y,ix,iu,iy)

x =
    0.0000
    1.0000
    1.0000
u =
    2
y =
    1.0000
    1.0000
dx =
   1.0e-015 *
   -0.2220
   -0.0227
    0.3331
```

Note that there may be no solution to equilibrium point problems. If that is the case, `trim` returns a solution that minimizes the maximum deviation from the desired result after first trying to set the derivatives to zero. For a description of the `trim` syntax, see `trim` in the online documentation.

Using Masks to Customize Blocks

Introduction	6-2
A Sample Masked Subsystem	6-3
Creating Mask Dialog Box Prompts	6-4
Creating the Block Description and Help Text	6-6
Creating the Block Icon	6-6
Summary	6-8
The Mask Editor: An Overview	6-9
The Initialization Page	6-10
Prompts and Associated Variables	6-10
Control Types	6-12
Default Values for Masked Block Parameters	6-14
Tunable Parameters	6-14
Initialization Commands	6-15
The Icon Page	6-18
Displaying Text on the Block Icon	6-18
Displaying Graphics on the Block Icon	6-20
Displaying Images on Masks	6-21
Displaying a Transfer Function on the Block Icon	6-22
Controlling Icon Properties	6-23
The Documentation Page	6-26
The Mask Type Field	6-26
The Block Description Field	6-26
The Mask Help Text Field	6-27

Introduction

Masking is a powerful Simulink feature that enables you to customize the dialog box and icon for a subsystem. With masking, you can:

- Simplify the use of your model by replacing many dialog boxes in a subsystem with a single one. Instead of requiring the user of the model to open each block and enter parameter values, those parameter values can be entered on the mask dialog box and passed to the blocks in the masked subsystem.
- Provide a more descriptive and helpful user interface by defining a dialog box with your own block description, parameter field labels, and help text.
- Define commands that compute variables whose values depend on block parameters.
- Create a block icon that depicts the subsystem's purpose.
- Prevent unintended modification of subsystems by hiding their contents behind a customized interface.
- Create dynamic dialogs.

A Sample Masked Subsystem

This simple subsystem models the equation for a line, y = mx + b.

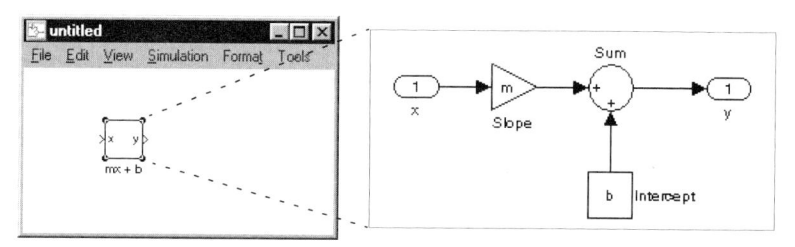

Ordinarily, when you double-click on a Subsystem block, the Subsystem block opens, displaying its blocks in a separate window. The mx + b subsystem contains a Gain block, named Slope, whose Gain parameter is specified as m, and a Constant block, named Intercept, whose Constant value parameter is specified as b. These parameters represent the slope and intercept of a line.

This example creates a custom dialog box and icon for the subsystem. One dialog box contains prompts for both the slope and the intercept. After you create the mask, double-click on the Subsystem block to open the mask dialog box. The mask dialog box and icon look like this.

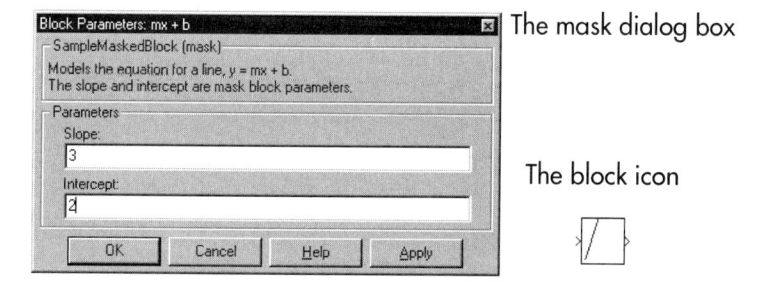

The mask dialog box

The block icon

A user enters values for **Slope** and **Intercept** into the mask dialog box. Simulink makes these values available to all the blocks in the underlying subsystem. Masking this subsystem creates a self-contained functional unit with its own application-specific parameters, Slope and Intercept. The mask maps these *mask parameters* to the generic parameters of the underlying blocks. The complexity of the subsystem is encapsulated by a new interface that has the look and feel of a built-in Simulink block.

6 Using Masks to Customize Blocks

To create a mask for this subsystem, you need to:

- Specify the prompts for the mask dialog box parameters. In this example, the mask dialog box has prompts for the slope and intercept.
- Specify the variable name used to store the value of each parameter.
- Enter the documentation of the block, consisting of the block description and the block help text.
- Specify the drawing command that creates the block icon.
- Specify the commands that provide the variables needed by the drawing command (there are none in this example).

Creating Mask Dialog Box Prompts

To create the mask for this subsystem, select the Subsystem block and choose **Mask Subsystem** from the **Edit** menu.

The mask dialog box shown at the beginning of this section is created largely on the **Initialization** page of the Mask Editor. For this sample model, it looks like this.

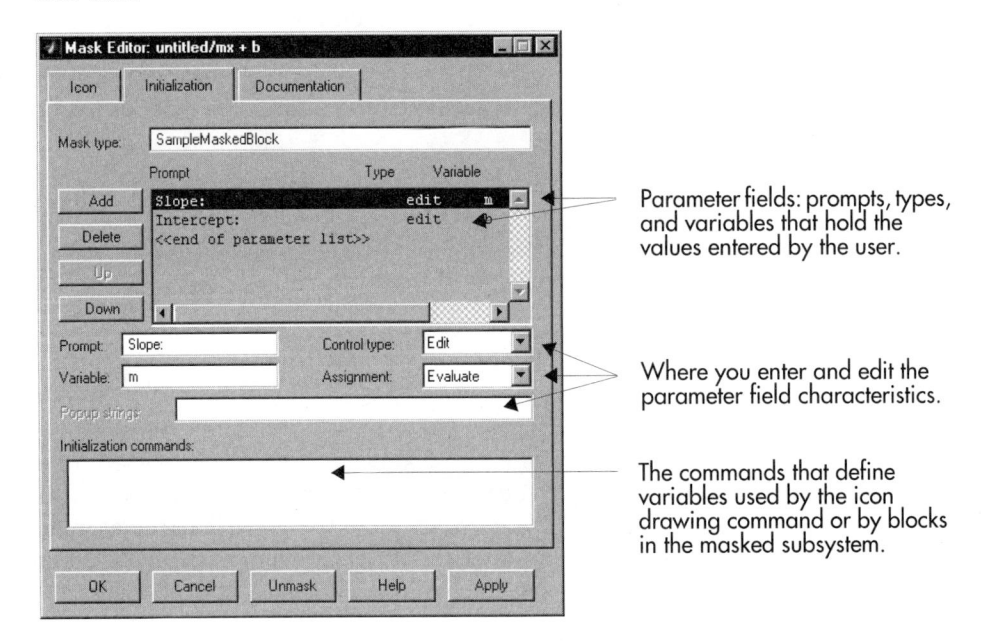

Parameter fields: prompts, types, and variables that hold the values entered by the user.

Where you enter and edit the parameter field characteristics.

The commands that define variables used by the icon drawing command or by blocks in the masked subsystem.

6-4

The Mask Editor enables you to specify these attributes of a mask parameter:

- The prompt – the text label that describes the parameter.
- The control type – the style of user interface control that determines how parameter values are entered or selected.
- The variable – the name of the variable that will store the parameter value.

Generally, it is convenient to refer to masked parameters by their prompts. In this example, the parameter associated with slope is referred to as the Slope parameter, and the parameter associated with intercept is referred to as the Intercept parameter.

The slope and intercept are defined as edit controls. This means that the user types values into edit fields in the mask dialog box. These values are stored in variables in the *mask workspace* (see "The Mask Workspace" on page 6-15). Masked blocks can access variables only in the mask workspace. In this example, the value entered for the slope is assigned to the variable m. The Slope block in the masked subsystem gets the value for the slope parameter from the mask workspace. This figure shows how the slope parameter definitions in the Mask Editor map to the actual mask dialog box parameters.

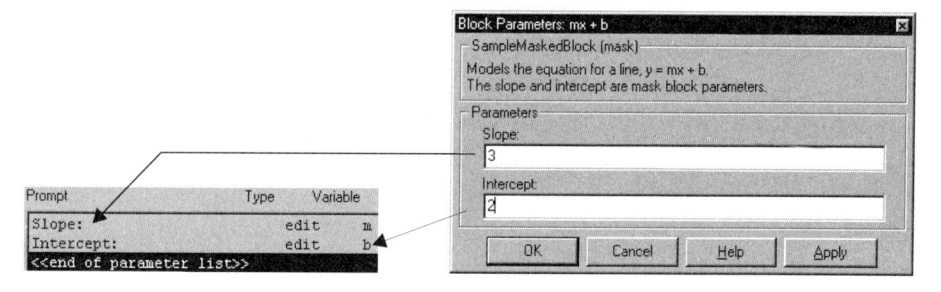

After you have created the mask parameters for slope and intercept, press the **OK** button. Then, double-click on the Subsystem block to open the newly constructed dialog box. Enter 3 for the **Slope** and 2 for the **Intercept** parameters.

Using Masks to Customize Blocks

Creating the Block Description and Help Text

The mask type, block description, and help text are defined on the **Documentation** page. For this sample masked block, the page looks like this.

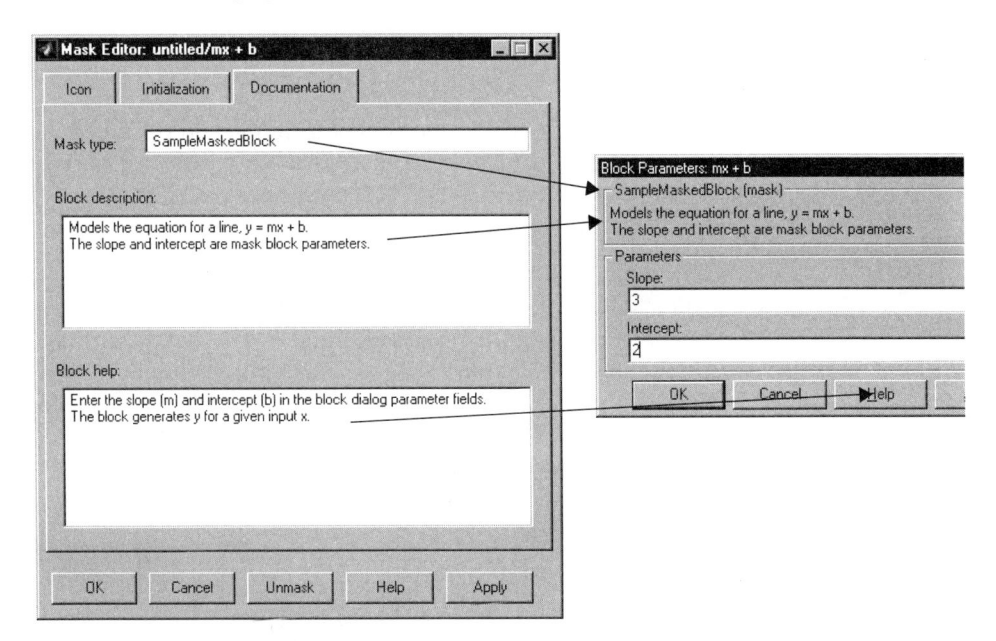

Creating the Block Icon

So far, we have created a customized dialog box for the mx + b subsystem. However, the Subsystem block still displays the generic Simulink subsystem icon. An appropriate icon for this masked block is a plot that indicates the slope of the line. For a slope of 3, that icon looks like this.

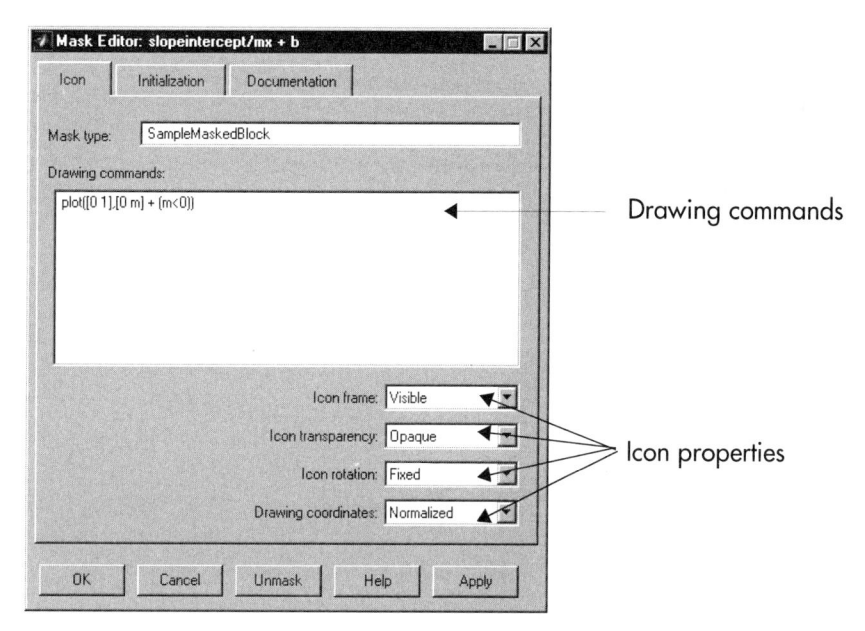

The block icon is defined on the **Icon** page. For this block, the **Icon** page looks like this.

Drawing commands

Icon properties

The drawing command plots a line from (0,0) to (0,m). If the slope is negative, Simulink shifts the line up by 1 to keep it within the visible drawing area of the block.

The drawing commands have access to all of the variables in the mask workspace. As you enter different values of slope, the icon updates the slope of the plotted line.

Select **Normalized** as the **Drawing coordinates** parameter, located at the bottom of the list of icon properties, to specify that the icon be drawn in a frame whose bottom-left corner is (0,0) and whose top-right corner is (1,1). This parameter is described later in this chapter.

Summary

This discussion of the steps involved in creating a sample mask introduced you to these tasks:

- Defining dialog box prompts and their characteristics
- Defining the masked block description and help text
- Defining the command that creates the masked block icon

The remainder of this chapter discusses the Mask Editor in more detail.

The Mask Editor: An Overview

To mask a subsystem (you can only mask Subsystem blocks), select the Subsystem block, then choose **Mask Subsystem** from the **Edit** menu. The Mask Editor appears. The Mask Editor consists of three pages, each handling a different aspect of the mask:

- The **Initialization** page enables you to define and describe mask dialog box parameter prompts, name the variables associated with the parameters, and specify initialization commands.
- The **Icon** page enables you to define the block icon.
- The **Documentation** page enables you to define the mask type and specify the block description and the block help.

Five buttons appear along the bottom of the Mask Editor:

- The **Ok** button applies the mask settings on all pages and closes the Mask Editor.
- The **Cancel** button closes the Mask Editor without applying any changes made since you last pressed the **Apply** button.
- The **Unmask** button deactivates the mask and closes the Mask Editor. The mask information is retained so that the mask can be reactivated. To reactivate the mask, select the block and choose **Create Mask**. The Mask Editor opens, displaying the previous settings. The inactive mask information is discarded when the model is closed and cannot be recovered.
- The **Help** button displays the contents of this chapter.
- The **Apply** button creates or changes the mask using the information that appears on all masking pages. The Mask Editor remains open.

To see the system under the mask without unmasking it, select the Subsystem block, then choose **Look Under Mask** from the **Edit** menu. This command opens the subsystem. The block's mask is not affected.

The Initialization Page

The mask interface enables a user of a masked system to enter parameter values for blocks within the masked system. You create the mask interface by defining prompts for parameter values on the **Initialization** page. The **Initialization** page for the mx+b sample masked system looks like this.

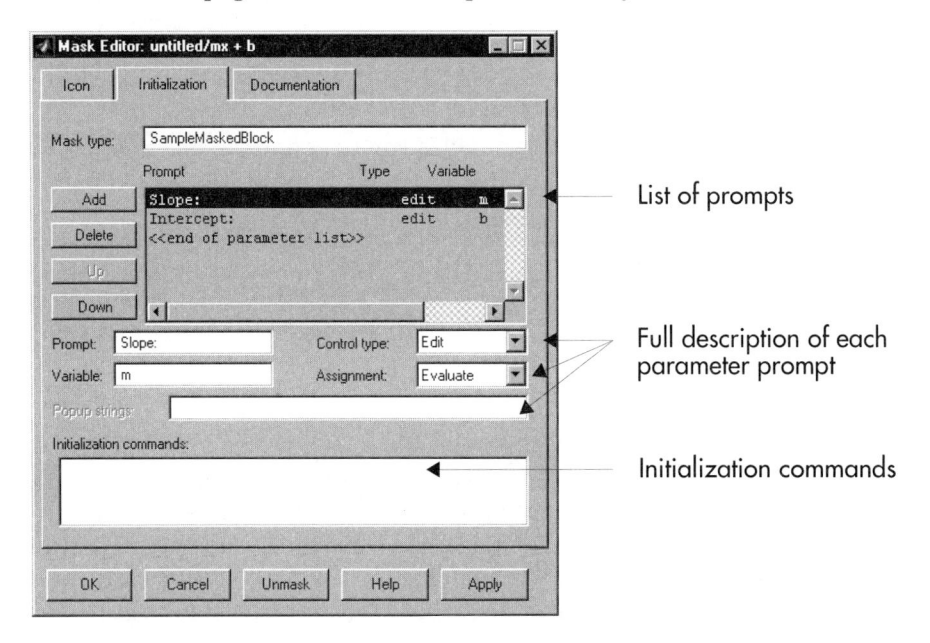

Prompts and Associated Variables

A *prompt* provides information that helps the user enter or select a value for a block parameter. Prompts appear on the mask dialog box in the order they appear in the **Prompt** list.

When you define a prompt, you also specify the variable that is to store the parameter value, choose the style of control for the prompt, and indicate how the value is to be stored in the variable.

If the **Assignment** type is **Evaluate**, the value entered by the user is evaluated by MATLAB before it is assigned to the variable. If the type is **Literal**, the value entered by the user is not evaluated, but is assigned to the variable as a string.

For example, if the user enters the string `gain` in an edit field and the **Assignment** type is **Evaluate**, the string `gain` is evaluated by MATLAB and the result is assigned to the variable. If the type is **Literal**, the string is not evaluated by MATLAB so the variable contains the string `'gain'`.

If you need both the string entered as well as the evaluated value, choose **Literal**. Then use the MATLAB `eval` command in the initialization commands. For example, if `LitVal` is the string `'gain'`, then to obtain the evaluated value, use the command

```
value = eval(LitVal)
```

In general, most parameters use an **Assignment** type of **Evaluate**.

Creating the First Prompt

To create the first prompt in the list, enter the prompt in the **Prompt** field, the variable that is to contain the parameter value in the **Variable** field, and choose a control style and an assignment type.

Inserting a Prompt

To insert a prompt in the list:

1 Select the prompt that appears immediately *below* where you want to insert the new prompt and click on the **Add** button to the left of the prompt list.

2 Enter the text for the prompt in the **Prompt** field. Enter the variable that is to hold the parameter value in the **Variable** field.

Editing a Prompt

To edit an existing prompt:

1 Select the prompt in the list. The prompt, variable name, control style, and assignment type appear in the fields below the list.

2 Edit the appropriate value. When you click the mouse outside the field or press the **Enter** or **Return** key, Simulink updates the prompt.

Deleting a Prompt

To delete a prompt from the list:

1 Select the prompt you want to delete.

2 Click on the **Delete** button to the left of the prompt list.

Moving a Prompt

To move a prompt in the list:

1 Select the prompt you want to move.

2 To move the prompt up one position in the prompt list, click on the **Up** button to the left of the prompt list. To move the prompt down one position, click on the **Down** button.

Control Types

Simulink enables you to choose how parameter values are entered or selected. You can create three styles of controls: edit fields, check boxes, and pop-up controls. For example, this figure shows the parameter area of a mask dialog box which uses all three styles of controls (with the pop-up control open).

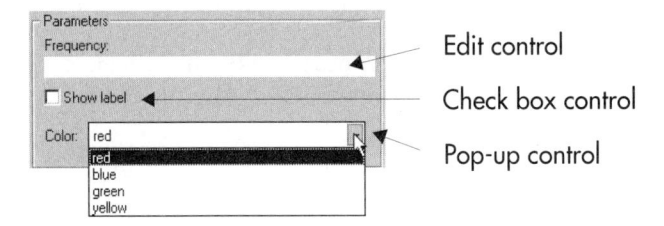

Defining an Edit Control

An *edit field* enables the user to enter a parameter value by typing it into a field. This figure shows how the prompt for the sample edit control was defined.

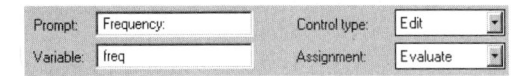

The value of the variable associated with the parameter (`freq`) is determined by the **Assignment** type defined for the prompt.

Assignment	Value
Evaluate	The result of evaluating the expression entered in the field.
Literal	The actual string entered in the field.

Defining a Check Box Control

A *check box* enables the user to choose between two alternatives by selecting or deselecting a check box. This figure shows how the sample check box control is defined.

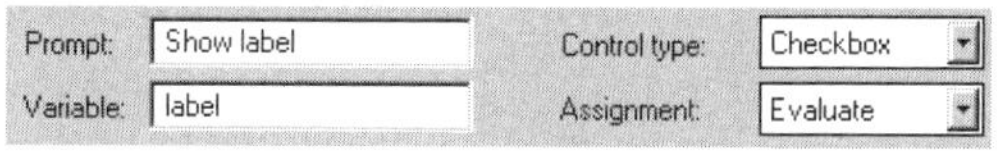

```
Prompt:    Show label          Control type:  Checkbox
Variable:  label               Assignment:    Evaluate
```

The value of the variable associated with the parameter (`label`) depends on whether the check box is selected and the **Assignment** type defined for the prompt.

Check Box	Evaluated Value	Literal Value
Checked	1	`'on'`
Not checked	0	`'off'`

Defining a Pop-Up Control

A *popup* enables the user to choose a parameter value from a list of possible values. You specify the list in the **Pop-up strings** field, separating items with a vertical line (|). This figure shows how the sample pop-up control is defined.

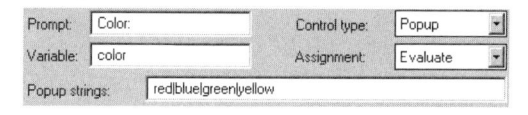

```
Prompt:        Color:              Control type:  Popup
Variable:      color               Assignment:    Evaluate
Popup strings: red|blue|green|yellow
```

The value of the variable associated with the parameter (color) depends on the item selected from the pop-up list and the **Assignment** type defined for the prompt.

Assignment	Value
Evaluate	The index of the value selected from the list, starting with 1. For example, if the third item is selected, the parameter value is 3.
Literal	A string that is the value selected. If the third item is selected, the parameter value is 'green'.

Default Values for Masked Block Parameters

To change default parameter values in a masked library block, follow these steps:

1 Unlock the library.

2 Open the block to access its dialog box, fill in the desired default values, and close the dialog box.

3 Save the library.

When the block is copied into a model and opened, the default values appear on the block's dialog box.

For more information about libraries, see the online documentation.

Tunable Parameters

A tunable parameter is a mask parameter that a user can modify at runtime. When you create a mask, all its parameters are tunable. You can subsequently disable or re-enable tuning of any of a mask's parameters via the MaskTunableValues parameter. The value of this parameter is a cell array of strings, each of which corresponds to one of a masked block's parameters. The first cell corresponds to the first parameter, the second cell to the second parameter, and so on. If a parameter is tunable, the value of the corresponding cell is on; otherwise, the value is off. To enable or disable tuning of a parameter, first get the cell array, using get_param. Then, set the corresponding cell to on or off and reset the MaskTunableValues parameter using set_param. For example, the following commands disable tuning of the first parameter of the currently selected masked block.

```
ca = get_param(gcb, 'MaskTunableValues');
ca(1) = 'off'
set_param(gcb, 'MaskTunableValues', ca)
```

After changing a block's tunable parameters, make the changes permanent by saving the block.

Initialization Commands

Initialization commands define variables that reside in the mask workspace. These variables can be used by all initialization commands defined for the mask, by blocks in the masked subsystem, and by commands that draw the block icon (drawing commands).

Simulink executes the initialization commands when:

- The model is loaded.
- The simulation is started or the block diagram is updated.
- The masked block is rotated.
- The block's icon needs to be redrawn and the plot commands depend on variables defined in the initialization commands.

Initialization commands are valid MATLAB expressions, consisting of MATLAB functions, operators, and variables defined in the mask workspace. Initialization commands cannot access base workspace variables. Terminate initialization commands with a semicolon to avoid echoing results to the command window.

The Mask Workspace

Simulink creates a local workspace, called a *mask workspace*, when either of the following occurs:

- The mask contains initialization commands.
- The mask defines prompts and associates variables with those prompts.

Masked blocks cannot access the base workspace or other mask workspaces.

6 Using Masks to Customize Blocks

The contents of a mask workspace include the variables associated with the mask's parameters and variables defined by initialization commands. The variables in the mask workspace can be accessed by the masked block. If the block is a subsystem, they can also be accessed by all blocks in the subsystem.

Mask workspaces are analogous to the local workspaces used by M-file functions. You can think of the expressions entered into the dialog boxes of the underlying blocks and the initialization commands entered on the Mask Editor as lines of an M-file function. Using this analogy, the local workspace for this "function" is the mask workspace.

In the mx + b example, described earlier in this chapter, the Mask Editor explicitly creates m and b in the mask workspace by associating a variable with a mask parameter. However, variables in the mask workspace are not explicitly assigned to blocks underneath the mask. Instead, blocks beneath the mask have access to all variables in the mask workspace. It may be instructive to think of the underlying blocks as "looking into" the mask workspace.

The figure below shows the mapping of values entered in the mask dialog box to variables in the mask workspace (indicated by the solid line) and the access of those variables by the underlying blocks (indicated by the dashed line).

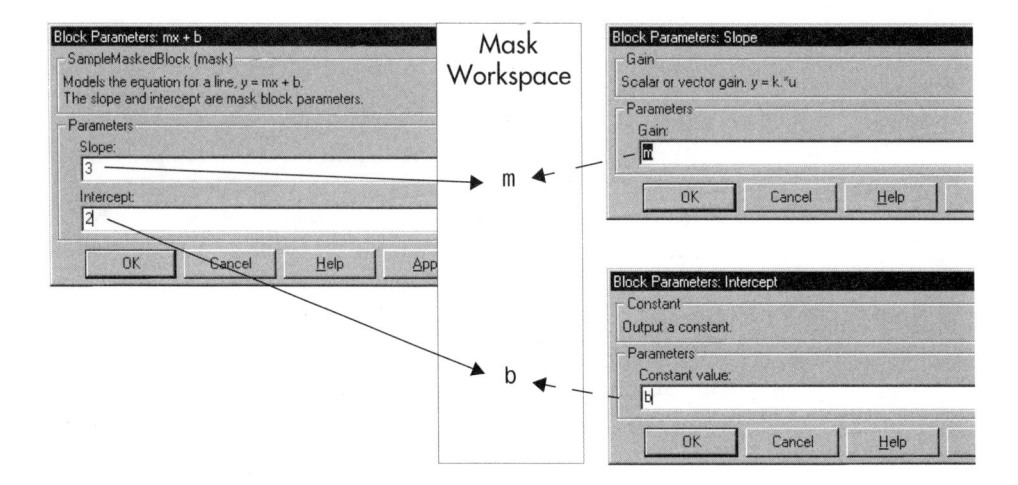

6-16

Debugging Initialization Commands

You can debug initialization commands in these ways:

- Specify an initialization command without a terminating semicolon to echo its results to the command window.
- Place a `keyboard` command in the initialization commands to stop execution and give control to the keyboard. For more information, see the help text for the `keyboard` command.
- Enter either of these commands in the MATLAB command window.

    ```
    dbstop if error
    dbstop if warning
    ```

    If an error occurs in the initialization commands, execution stops and you can examine the mask workspace. For more information, see the help text for the `dbstop` command.

The Icon Page

The **Icon** page enables you to customize the masked block's icon. You create a custom icon by specifying commands in the **Drawing commands** field. You can create icons that show descriptive text, state equations, images, and graphics. This figure shows the **Icon** page.

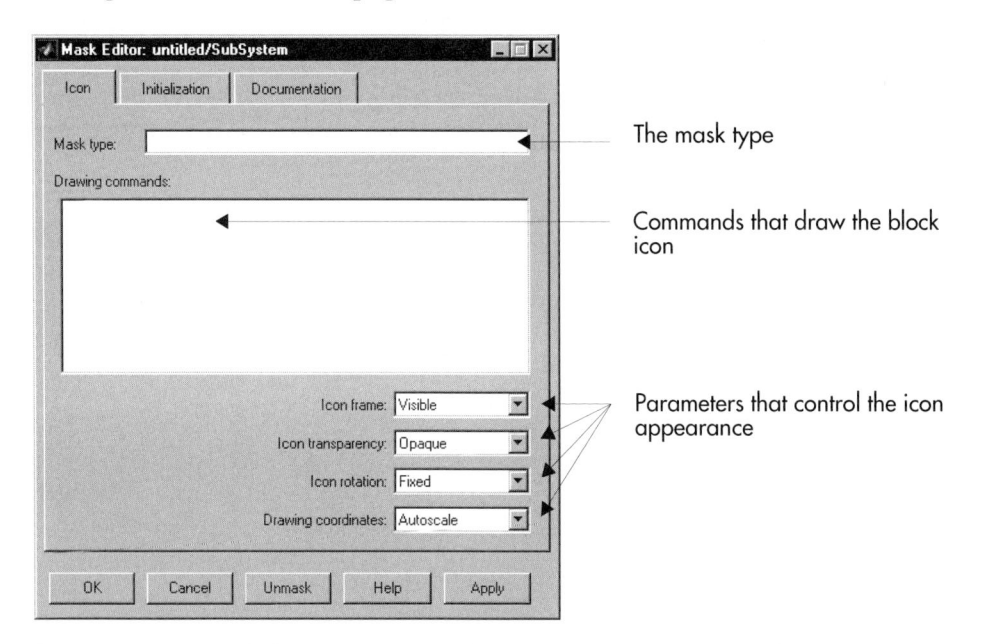

Drawing commands have access to all variables in the mask workspace.

Drawing commands can display text, one or more plots, or show a transfer function. If you enter more than one command, the results of the commands are drawn on the icon in the order the commands appear.

Displaying Text on the Block Icon

To display text on the icon, enter one of these drawing commands.

```
disp('text') or disp(variablename)

text(x, y, 'text')
text(x, y, stringvariablename)
```

```
text(x, y, text, 'horizontalAlignment', halign,
'verticalAlignment', valign)

fprintf('text') or fprintf('format', variablename)

port_label(port_type, port_number, label)
```

The `disp` command displays `text` or the contents of `variablename` centered on the icon.

The `text` command places a character string (`text` or the contents of `stringvariablename`) at a location specified by the point (x,y). The units depend on the **Drawing coordinates** parameter. For more information, see "Controlling Icon Properties" on page 6-23.

You can optionally specify the horizontal and/or vertical alignment of the text relative to the point (x, y) in the `text` command. For example, the command

```
text(0.5, 0.5, 'foobar', 'horizontalAlignment', 'center')
```

centers `foobar` in the icon.

The `text` command offers the following horizontal alignment options.

Option	Aligns
left	The left end of the text at the specified point.
right	The right end of the text at the specified point.
center	The center of the text at the specified point.

The `text` command offers the following vertical alignment options.

Option	Aligns
base	The baseline of the text at the specified point.
bottom	The bottom line of the text at the specified point.
middle	The midline of the text at the specified point.

Option	Aligns
cap	The capitals line of the text at the specified point.
top	The top of the text at the specified point.

The `fprintf` command displays formatted text centered on the icon and can display `text` along with the contents of `variablename`.

Note While these commands are identical in name to their corresponding MATLAB functions, they provide only the functionality described above.

To display more than one line of text, use `\n` to indicate a line break. For example, the figure below shows two samples of the `disp` command.

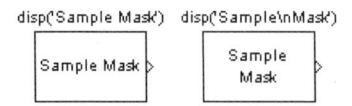

The `port_label` command lets you specify the labels of ports displayed on the icon. The command's syntax is

```
port_label(port_type, port_number, label)
```

where `port_type` is either `'input'` or `'output'`, `port_number` is an integer, and `label` is a string specifying the port's label. For example, the command

```
port_label('input', 1, 'a')
```

defines a as the label of input port 1.

Displaying Graphics on the Block Icon

You can display plots on your masked block icon by entering one or more `plot` commands. You can use these forms of the plot command.

```
plot(Y);
plot(X1,Y1,X2,Y2,...);
```

`plot(Y)` plots, for a vector Y, each element against its index. If Y is a matrix, it plots each column of the matrix as though it were a vector.

`plot(X1,Y1,X2,Y2,...)` plots the vectors Y1 against X1, Y2 against X2, and so on. Vector pairs must be the same length and the list must consist of an even number of vectors.

For example, this command generates the plot that appears on the icon for the Ramp block, in the Sources library. The icon appears below the command.

```
plot([0 1 5], [0 0 4])
```

Plot commands can include `NaN` and `inf` values. When `NaN`s or `inf`s are encountered, Simulink stops drawing, then begins redrawing at the next numbers that are not `NaN` or `inf`.

The appearance of the plot on the icon depends on the value of the **Drawing coordinates** parameter. For more information, see "Controlling Icon Properties" on page 6-23.

Simulink displays three question marks (? ? ?) in the block icon and issues warnings in these situations:

- When the values for the parameters used in the drawing commands are not yet defined (for example, when the mask is first created and values have not yet been entered into the mask dialog box).
- When a masked block parameter or drawing command is entered incorrectly.

Displaying Images on Masks

The masked dialog functions, `image` and `patch`, enable you to display bitmapped images and draw patches on masked block icons.

`image(a)` displays the image a where a is an M by N by 3 array of RGB values. You can use the MATLAB commands, `imread` and `ind2rgb`, to read and convert bitmap files to the necessary matrix format. For example,

```
image(imread('icon.tif'))
```

reads the icon image from a TIFF file named `icon.tif` in the MATLAB path.

`image(a, [x, y, w, h])` creates the image at the specified position relative to the lower left corner of the mask.

`image(a, [x, y, w, h], rotation)` allows you to specify whether the image rotates (`'on'`) or remains stationary (`'off'`) as the icon rotates. The default is `'off'`.

`patch(x, y)` creates a solid patch having the shape specified by the coordinate vectors x and y. The patch's color is the current foreground color.

`patch(x, y, [r g b])` creates a solid patch of the color specified by the vector [r g b], where r is the red component, g the green, and b the blue. For example,

```
patch([0 .5 1], [0 1 0], [1 0 0])
```

creates a red triangle on the mask's icon.

Displaying a Transfer Function on the Block Icon

To display a transfer function equation in the block icon, enter the following command in the **Drawing commands** field.

```
dpoly(num, den)
dpoly(num, den, 'character')
```

num and den are vectors of transfer function numerator and denominator coefficients, typically defined using initialization commands. The equation is expressed in terms of the specified character. The default is s. When the icon is drawn, the initialization commands are executed and the resulting equation is drawn on the icon.

- To display a continuous transfer function in descending powers of s, enter

    ```
    dpoly(num, den)
    ```

    For example, for num = [0 0 1]; and den = [1 2 1]; the icon looks like this.

    $$\frac{1}{s^2+2s+1}$$

- To display a discrete transfer function in descending powers of z, enter

    ```
    dpoly(num, den, 'z')
    ```

    For example, for num = [0 0 1]; and den = [1 2 1]; the icon looks like this.

    $$\frac{1}{z^2+2z+1}$$

- To display a discrete transfer function in ascending powers of $1/z$, enter

  `dpoly(num, den, 'z-')`

  For example, for num and den as defined above, the icon looks like this.

  $$\frac{z^{-2}}{1+2z^{-1}+z^{-2}}$$

- To display a zero-pole gain transfer function, enter

  `droots(z, p, k)`

  For example, the above command creates this icon for these values.

  `z = []; p = [-1 -1]; k = 1;`

  $$\frac{1}{(s+1)(s+1)}$$

  You can add a fourth argument (`'z'` or `'z-'`) to express the equation in terms of z or $1/z$.

If the parameters are not defined or have no values when you create the icon, Simulink displays three question marks (? ? ?) in the icon. When the parameter values are entered in the mask dialog box, Simulink evaluates the transfer function and displays the resulting equation in the icon.

Controlling Icon Properties

You can control a masked block's icon properties by selecting among the choices below the **Drawing commands** field.

Icon Frame

The icon frame is the rectangle that encloses the block. You can choose to show or hide the frame by setting the **Icon frame** parameter to **Visible** or **Invisible**. The default is to make the icon frame visible. For example, this figure shows visible and invisible icon frames for an AND gate block.

Icon Transparency

The icon can be set to **Opaque** or **Transparent**, either hiding or showing what is underneath the icon. **Opaque**, the default, covers information Simulink draws, such as port labels. This figure shows opaque and transparent icons for an AND gate block. Notice the text on the transparent icon.

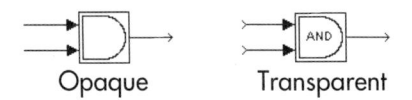

Opaque   Transparent

Icon Rotation

When the block is rotated or flipped, you can choose whether to rotate or flip the icon, or to have it remain fixed in its original orientation. The default is not to rotate the icon. The icon rotation is consistent with block port rotation. This figure shows the results of choosing **Fixed** and **Rotates** icon rotation when the AND gate block is rotated.

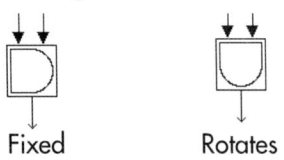

Fixed   Rotates

Drawing Coordinates

This parameter controls the coordinate system used by the drawing commands. This parameter applies only to `plot` and `text` drawing commands. You can select from among these choices: **Autoscale**, **Normalized**, and **Pixel**.

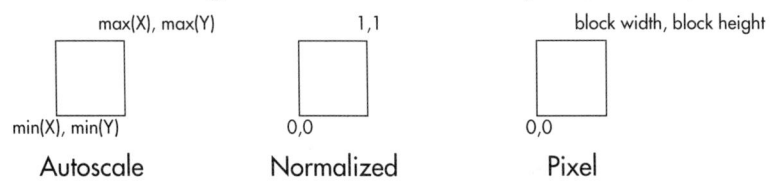

Autoscale: max(X), max(Y) / min(X), min(Y)
Normalized: 1,1 / 0,0
Pixel: block width, block height / 0,0

- **Autoscale** automatically scales the icon within the block frame. When the block is resized, the icon is also resized. For example, this figure shows the icon drawn using these vectors.
  ```
  X = [0 2 3 4 9]; Y = [4 6 3 5 8];
  ```

  The lower-left corner of the block frame is (0,3) and the upper-right corner is (9,8). The range of the x-axis is 9 (from 0 to 9), while the range of the y-axis is 5 (from 3 to 8).

- **Normalized** draws the icon within a block frame whose bottom-left corner is (0,0) and whose top right corner is (1,1). Only X and Y values between 0 and 1 appear. When the block is resized, the icon is also resized. For example, this figure shows the icon drawn using these vectors.
  ```
  X = [.0 .2 .3 .4 .9]; Y = [.4 .6 .3 .5 .8];
  ```

- **Pixel** draws the icon with X and Y values expressed in pixels. The icon is not automatically resized when the block is resized. To force the icon to resize with the block, define the drawing commands in terms of the block size.

  This example demonstrates how to create an improved icon for the mx + b sample masked subsystem discussed earlier in this chapter. These initialization commands define the data that enables the drawing command to produce an accurate icon regardless of the shape of the block.
  ```
  pos = get_param(gcb, 'Position');
  width = pos(3) - pos(1); height = pos(4) - pos(2);
  x = [0, width];
  if (m >= 0), y = [0, (m*width)]; end
  if (m < 0),  y = [height, (height + (m*width))]; end
  ```

  The drawing command that generates this icon is plot(x,y).

The Documentation Page

The **Documentation** page enables you to define or modify the type, description, and help text for a masked block. This figure shows how fields on the **Documentation** page correspond to the mx+b sample mask block's dialog box.

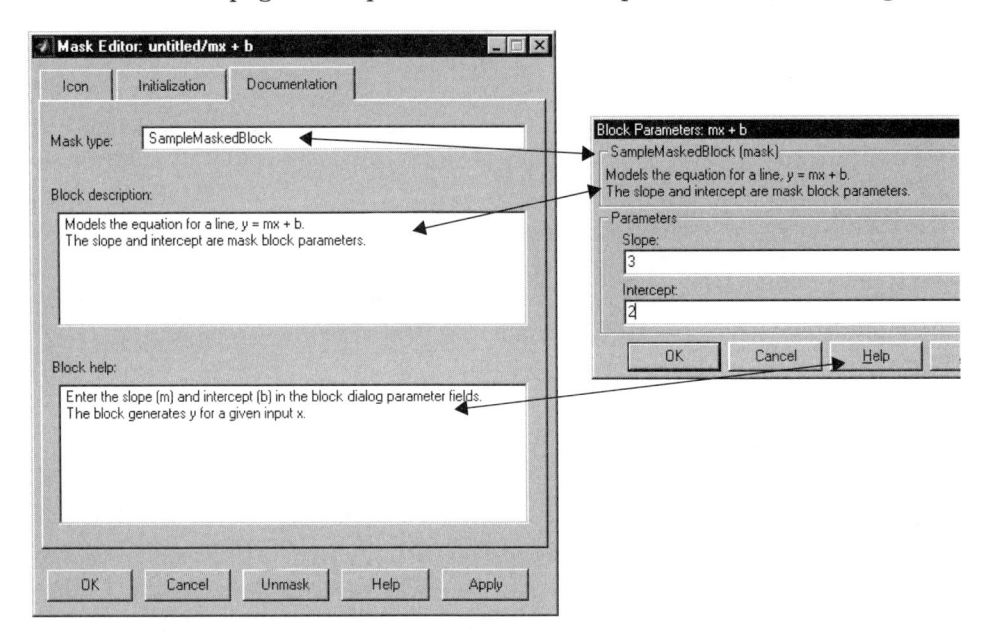

The Mask Type Field

The mask type is a block classification used only for purposes of documentation. It appears in the block's dialog box and on all Mask Editor pages for the block. You can choose any name you want for the mask type. When Simulink creates the block's dialog box, it adds "(mask)" after the mask type to differentiate masked blocks from built-in blocks.

The Block Description Field

The block description is informative text that appears in the block's dialog box in the frame under the mask type. If you are designing a system for others to use, this is a good place to describe the block's purpose or function.

Simulink automatically wraps long lines of text. You can force line breaks by using the **Enter** or **Return** key.

The Mask Help Text Field

You can provide help text that gets displayed when the **Help** button is pressed on the masked block's dialog box. If you create models for others to use, this is a good place to explain how the block works and how to enter its parameters.

You can include user-written documentation for a masked block's help. You can specify any of the following for the masked block help text:

- URL specification (a string starting with `http:`, `www`, `file:`, `ftp:`, or `mailto:`)
- `web` command (launches a browser)
- `eval` command (evaluates a MATLAB string)
- Static text displayed in the Web browser

Simulink examines the first line of the masked block help text. If it detects a URL specification, `web` command, or `eval` command, it accesses the block help as directed; otherwise, the full contents of the masked block help text are displayed in the browser.

These examples illustrate several acceptable commands.

```
web([docroot '/My Blockset Doc/' get_param(gcb,'MaskType') '.html'])
eval('!Word My_Spec.doc')
http://www.mathworks.com
file:///c:/mydir/helpdoc.html
www.mathworks.com
```

Simulink automatically wraps long lines of text.

Using Masks to Customize Blocks

Additional Topics

How Simulink Works 7-2
Zero Crossings 7-3
Algebraic Loops 7-7
Invariant Constants 7-11

Discrete-Time Systems 7-13
Discrete Blocks 7-13
Sample Time .7-13
Purely Discrete Systems 7-13
Multirate Systems 7-14
Sample Time Colors 7-15
Mixed Continuous and Discrete Systems 7-17

How Simulink Works

Each block within a Simulink model has these general characteristics: a vector of inputs, u, a vector of outputs, y, and a vector of states, x.

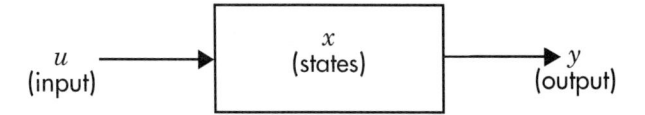

$$u \text{ (input)} \longrightarrow \boxed{x \text{ (states)}} \longrightarrow y \text{ (output)}$$

The state vector may consist of continuous states, discrete states, or a combination of both. The mathematical relationships between these quantities are expressed by these equations.

$$y = f_o(t, x, u) \qquad \text{Output}$$
$$x_{d_{k+1}} = f_u(t, x, u) \qquad \text{Update}$$
$$x'_c = f_d(t, x, u) \qquad \text{Derivative}$$

$$\text{where } x = \begin{bmatrix} x_c \\ x_{d_k} \end{bmatrix}$$

Simulation consists of two phases: initialization and simulation. During the initialization phase:

1 The block parameters are passed to MATLAB for evaluation. The resulting numerical values are used as the actual block parameters.

2 The model hierarchy is flattened. Each subsystem that is not a conditionally executed subsystem is replaced by the blocks it contains.

3 Blocks are sorted into the order in which they need to be updated. The sorting algorithm constructs a list such that any block with direct feedthrough is not updated until the blocks driving its inputs are updated. It is during this step that algebraic loops are detected. For more information about algebraic loops, see "Algebraic Loops" on page 7-7.

4 The connections between blocks are checked to ensure that the vector length of the output of each block is the same as the input expected by the blocks it drives.

Now the simulation is ready to run. A model is simulated using numerical integration. Each of the supplied ODE solvers (simulation methods) depends on the ability of the model to provide the derivatives of its continuous states. Calculating these derivatives is a two-step process. First, each block's output is calculated in the order determined during the sorting. Then, in a second pass, each block calculates its derivatives based on the current time, its inputs, and its states. The resulting derivative vector is returned to the solver, which uses it to compute a new state vector at the next time point. Once a new state vector is calculated, the sampled data blocks and Scope blocks are updated.

Zero Crossings

Simulink uses zero crossings to detect discontinuities in continuous signals. Zero crossings play an important role in:

- The handling of state events
- The accurate integration of discontinuous signals

State Event Handling

A system experiences a *state event* when a change in the value of a state causes the system to undergo a distinct change. A simple example of a state event is a bouncing ball hitting the floor. When simulating such a system using a variable-step solver, the solver typically does not take steps that exactly correspond to the times that the ball makes contact with the floor. As a result, the ball is likely to overshoot the contact point, which results in the ball penetrating the floor.

Simulink uses zero crossings to ensure that time steps occur exactly (within machine precision) at the time state events occur. Because time steps occur at the exact time of contact, the simulation produces no overshoot and the transition from negative to positive velocity is extremely sharp (that is, there is no rounding of corners at the discontinuity). To see a bouncing ball demo, type bounce at the MATLAB prompt.

Integration of Discontinuous Signals

Numerical integration routines are formulated on the assumption that the signals they are integrating are continuous and have continuous derivatives. If a discontinuity (state event) is encountered during an integration step, Simulink uses zero crossing detection to find the time at which the discontinuity occurs. An integration step is then taken up to the left edge of the discontinuity. Finally, Simulink steps over the discontinuity and begins a new integration step on the next piece-wise continuous portion of the signal.

Implementation Details

An example of a Simulink block that uses zero crossings is the Saturation block. Zero crossings detect these state events in the Saturation block:

- The input signal reaches the upper limit.
- The input signal leaves the upper limit.
- The input signal reaches the lower limit.
- The input signal leaves the lower limit.

Simulink blocks that define their own state events are considered to have *intrinsic zero crossings*. If you need explicit notification of a zero crossing event, use the Hit Crossing block. See "Blocks with Zero Crossings" on page 7-6 for a list of blocks that incorporate zero crossings.

The detection of a state event depends on the construction of an internal zero crossing signal. This signal is not accessible by the block diagram. For the Saturation block, the signal that is used to detect zero crossings for the upper limit is `zcSignal = UpperLimit - u`, where u is the input signal.

Zero crossing signals have a direction attribute, which can have these values:

- *rising* – a zero crossing occurs when a signal rises to or through zero, or when a signal leaves zero and becomes positive.
- *falling* – a zero crossing occurs when a signal falls to or through zero, or when a signal leaves zero and becomes negative.
- *either* – a zero crossing occurs if either a rising or falling condition occurs.

For the Saturation block's upper limit, the direction of the zero crossing is *either*. This enables the entering and leaving saturation events to be detected using the same zero crossing signal.

If the error tolerances are too large, it is possible for Simulink to fail to detect a zero crossing. For example, if a zero crossing occurs within a time step, but the values at the beginning and end of the step do not indicate a sign change, the solver will step over the crossing without detecting it.

This figure shows a signal that crosses zero. In the first instance, the integrator "steps over" the event. In the second, the solver detects the event.

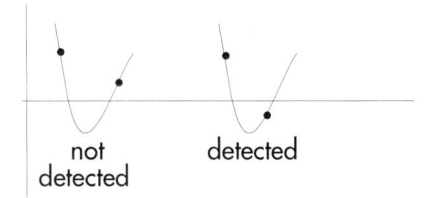

If you suspect this is happening, tighten the error tolerances to ensure that the solver takes small enough steps. For more information, see "Error Tolerances" on page 4–13.

Caveat

It is possible to create models that exhibit high frequency fluctuations about a discontinuity (chattering). Such systems typically are not physically realizable; a mass-less spring, for example. Because chattering causes repeated detection of zero crossings, the step sizes of the simulation become very small, essentially halting the simulation.

If you suspect that this behavior applies to your model, you can disable zero crossings by selecting the **Disable zero crossing detection** check box on the **Diagnostics** page of the **Simulation Parameters** dialog box. Although disabling zero crossing detection may alleviate the symptoms of this problem, you no longer benefit from the increased accuracy that zero crossing detection provides. A better solution is to try to identify the source of the underlying problem in the model.

Blocks with Zero Crossings

Table 7-1: Blocks with Intrinsic Zero Crossings

Block	Description of Zero Crossing
Abs	One: to detect when the input signal crosses zero in either the rising or falling direction.
Backlash	Two: one to detect when the upper threshold is engaged, and one to detect when the lower threshold is engaged.
Dead Zone	Two: one to detect when the dead zone is entered (the input signal minus the lower limit), and one to detect when the dead zone is exited (the input signal minus the upper limit).
Hit Crossing	One: to detect when the input crosses the threshold. These zero crossings are not affected by the **Disable zero crossing detection** check box in the **Simulation Parameters** dialog box.
Integrator	If the reset port is present, to detect when a reset occurs. If the output is limited, there are three zero crossings: one to detect when the upper saturation limit is reached, one to detect when the lower saturation limit is reached, and one to detect when saturation is left.
MinMax	One: for each element of the output vector, to detect when an input signal is the new minimum or maximum
Relay	One: if the relay is off, to detect the switch on point. If the relay is on, to detect the switch off point.
Relational Operator	One: to detect when the output changes.
Saturation	Two: one to detect when the upper limit is reached or left, and one to detect when the lower limit is reached or left.
Sign	One: to detect when the input crosses through zero.
Step	One: to detect the step time.

Table 7-1: Blocks with Intrinsic Zero Crossings (Continued)

Block	Description of Zero Crossing
Subsystem	For conditionally executed subsystems: one for the enable port if present, and one for the trigger port, if present.
Switch	One: to detect when the switch condition occurs.

Algebraic Loops

Some Simulink blocks have input ports with *direct feedthrough*. This means that the output of these blocks cannot be computed without knowing the values of the signals entering the blocks at these input ports. Some examples of blocks with direct feedthrough inputs are:

- The Elementary Math block
- The Gain block
- The Integrator block's initial condition ports
- The Product block
- The State-Space block when there is a nonzero D matrix
- The Sum block
- The Transfer Fcn block when the numerator and denominator are of the same order
- The Zero-Pole block when there are as many zeros as poles

To determine whether a block has direct feedthrough, consult the Characteristics table that describes the block, in the online documentation.

An *algebraic loop* generally occurs when an input port with direct feedthrough is driven by the output of the same block, either directly, or by a feedback path through other blocks with direct feedthrough. (See "Nonalgebraic Direct-Feedthrough Loops" on page 7-9 for an example of an exception to this general rule.) An example of an algebraic loop is this simple scalar loop.

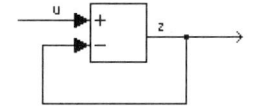

7 Additional Topics

Mathematically, this loop implies that the output of the Sum block is an algebraic state z constrained to equal the first input u minus z (i.e. $z = u - z$). The solution of this simple loop is $z = u/2$, but most algebraic loops cannot be solved by inspection. It is easy to create vector algebraic loops with multiple algebraic state variables $z1$, $z2$, etc., as shown in this model.

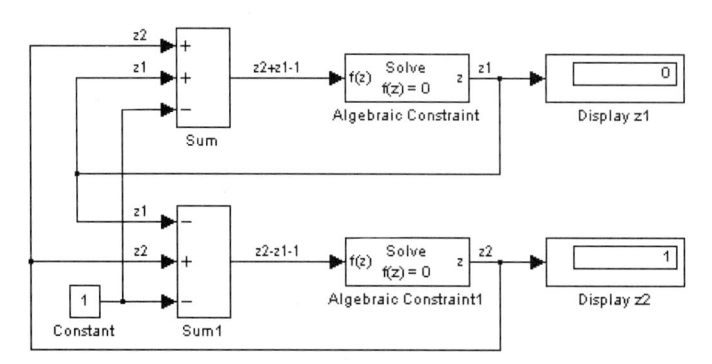

The Algebraic Constraint block (see Algebraic Constraint in the online documentation) is a convenient way to model algebraic equations and specify initial guesses. The Algebraic Constraint block constrains its input signal $F(z)$ to zero and outputs an algebraic state z. This block outputs the value necessary to produce a zero at the input. The output must affect the input through some feedback path. You can provide an initial guess of the algebraic state value in the block's dialog box to improve algebraic loop solver efficiency.

A scalar algebraic loop represents a scalar algebraic equation or constraint of the form $F(z) = 0$, where z is the output of one of the blocks in the loop and the function F consists of the feedback path through the other blocks in the loop to the input of the block. In the simple one-block example shown on the previous page, $F(z) = z - (u - z)$. In the vector loop example shown above, the equations are

$z2 + z1 - 1 = 0$
$z2 - z1 - 1 = 0$

Algebraic loops arise when a model includes an algebraic constraint $F(z) = 0$. This constraint may arise as a consequence of the physical interconnectivity of the system you are modeling, or it may arise because you are specifically trying to model a differential/algebraic system (DAE).

When a model contains an algebraic loop, Simulink calls a loop solving routine at each time step. The loop solver performs iterations to determine the solution to the problem (if it can). As a result, models with algebraic loops run slower than models without them.

To solve $F(z) = 0$, the Simulink loop solver uses Newton's method with weak line search and rank-one updates to a Jacobian matrix of partial derivatives. Although the method is robust, it is possible to create loops for which the loop solver will not converge without a good initial guess for the algebraic states z. You can specify an initial guess for a line in an algebraic loop by placing an IC block (which is normally used to specify an initial condition for a signal) on that line. As shown above, another way to specify an initial guess for a line in an algebraic loop is to use an Algebraic Constraint block.

Whenever possible, use an IC block or an Algebraic Constraint block to specify an initial guess for the algebraic state variables in a loop.

Nonalgebraic Direct-Feedthrough Loops

There are exceptions to the general rule that all loops comprising direct-feedthrough blocks are algebraic. The exceptions are:

- Loops involving triggered subsystems
- A loop from the output to the reset port of an integrator

In the case of a triggered subsystem, a solver can safely assume that the subsystem's inputs are stable at the time of the trigger. This allows use of the output from a previous time step to compute the input at the current time step, thus eliminating the need for an algebraic loop solver.

Additional Topics

Consider, for example, the following system.

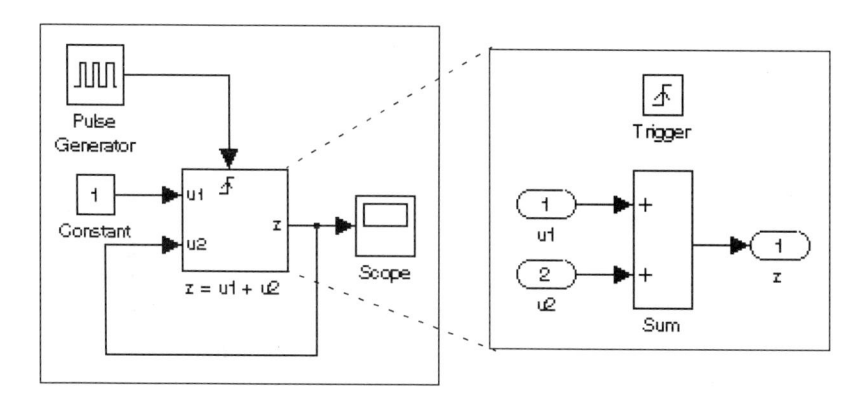

This system effectively solves the equation

$$z = z + 1$$

where u is the value of z the last time the subsystem was triggered. The output of the system is a staircase function as illustrated by the display on the system's scope.

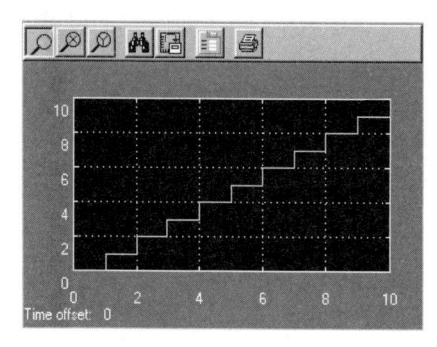

Now consider the effect of removing the trigger from the system shown in the previous example.

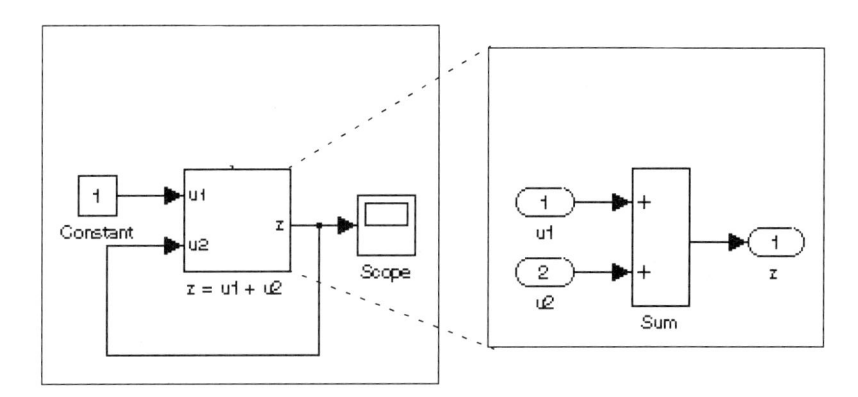

In this case, the input at the u2 port of the adder subsystem is equal to the subsystem's output at the current time step for every time step. The mathematical representation of this system

    z = z + 1

reveals that it has no mathematically valid solution.

Invariant Constants

Blocks either have explicitly defined sample times or inherit their sample times from blocks that feed them or are fed by them.

Simulink assigns Constant blocks a sample time of infinity, also referred to as a *constant sample time*. Other blocks have constant sample time if they receive their input from a Constant block and do not inherit the sample time of another block. This means that the output of these blocks does not change during the simulation unless the parameters are explicitly modified by the model user.

For example, in this model, both the Constant and Gain blocks have constant sample time.

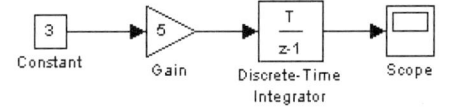

Because Simulink supports the ability to change block parameters during a simulation, all blocks, even blocks having constant sample time, must generate their output at the model's effective sample time.

Because of this feature, *all* blocks compute their output at each sample time hit, or, in the case of purely continuous systems, at every simulation step. For blocks having constant sample time whose parameters do not change during a simulation, evaluating these blocks during the simulation is inefficient and slows down the simulation.

You can set the InvariantConstants parameter to remove all blocks having constant sample times from the simulation "loop." The effect of this feature is twofold: first, parameters for these blocks cannot be changed during a simulation; and second, simulation speed is improved. The speed improvement depends on model complexity, the number of blocks with constant sample time, and the effective sampling rate of the simulation.

You can set the parameter for your model by entering this command.

```
set_param('model_name', 'InvariantConstants', 'on')
```

You can turn off the feature by issuing the command again, assigning the parameter the value of `'off'`.

You can determine which blocks have constant sample time by selecting **Sample Time Colors** from the **Format** menu. Blocks having constant sample time are colored magenta.

Discrete-Time Systems

Simulink has the ability to simulate discrete (sampled data) systems. Models can be *multirate*; that is, they can contain blocks that are sampled at different rates. Models can also be *hybrid*, containing a mixture of discrete and continuous blocks.

Discrete Blocks

Each of the discrete blocks has a built-in sampler at its input, and a zero-order hold at its output. When the discrete blocks are mixed with continuous blocks, the output of the discrete blocks between sample times is held constant. The outputs of the discrete blocks are updated only at times that correspond to sample hits.

Sample Time

The **Sample time** parameter sets the sample time at which a discrete block's states are updated. Normally, the sample time is set to a scalar variable; however, it is possible to specify an offset time (or skew) by specifying a two-element vector in this field.

For example, specifying the **Sample time** parameter as the vector [Ts,offset] sets the sample time to Ts and the offset value to offset. The discrete block is updated on integer multiples of the sample time and offset values only

```
t = n * Ts + offset
```

where n is an integer and offset can be positive or negative, but less than the sample time. The offset is useful if some discrete blocks must be updated sooner or later than others.

You cannot change the sample time of a block while a simulation is running. If you want to change a block's sample time, you must stop and restart the simulation for the change to take effect.

Purely Discrete Systems

Purely discrete systems can be simulated using any of the solvers; there is no difference in the solutions. To generate output points only at the sample hits, choose one of the discrete solvers.

Multirate Systems

Multirate systems contain blocks that are sampled at different rates. These systems can be modeled with discrete blocks or both discrete and continuous blocks. For example, consider this simple multirate discrete model.

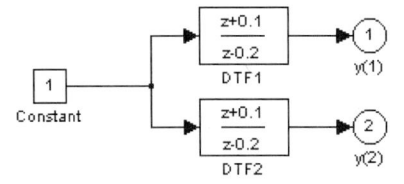

For this example the DTF1 Discrete Transfer Fcn block's **Sample time** is set to [1 0.1], which gives it an offset of 0.1. The DTF2 Discrete Transfer Fcn block's **Sample time** is set to 0.7, with no offset.

Starting the simulation and plotting the outputs using the stairs function

```
[t,x,y] = sim('multirate', 3);
stairs(t,y)
```

produces this plot.

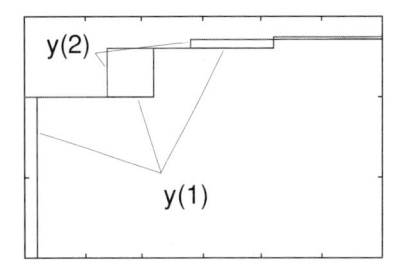

For the DTF1 block, which has an offset of 0.1, there is no output until t = 0.1. Because the initial conditions of the transfer functions are zero, the output of DTF1, y(1), is zero before this time.

Sample Time Colors

Simulink identifies different sample rates in a model using the sample time color feature, which shows sample rates by applying the color scheme shown in this table.

Table 7-2: Sample Time Colors

Color	Use
Black	Continuous blocks
Magenta	Constant blocks
Yellow	Hybrid (subsystems grouping blocks, or Mux or Demux blocks grouping signals with varying sample times)
Red	Fastest discrete sample time
Green	Second fastest discrete sample time
Blue	Third fastest discrete sample time
Light Blue	Fourth fastest discrete sample time
Dark Green	Fifth fastest discrete sample time
Cyan	Triggered sample time
Gray	Fixed in minor step

To understand how this feature works, it is important to be familiar with Simulink's Sample Time Propagation Engine (STPE). The figure below illustrates a Discrete Filter block with a sample time of Ts driving a Gain block. Because the Gain block's output is simply the input multiplied by a constant, its output changes at the same rate as the filter. In other words, the Gain block has an effective sample rate equal to that of the filter's sample rate. This is the fundamental mechanism behind the STPE.

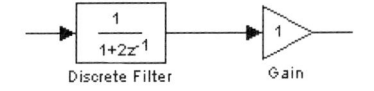

Additional Topics

To enable the sample time colors feature, select **Sample Time Colors** from the **Format** menu.

Simulink does not automatically recolor the model with each change you make to it, so you must select **Update Diagram** from the **Edit** menu to explicitly update the model coloration. To return to your original coloring, disable sample time coloration by again choosing **Sample Time Colors**.

When using sample time colors, the color assigned to each block depends on its sample time with respect to other sample times in the model.

Simulink sets sample times for individual blocks according to these rules:

- Continuous blocks (e.g., Integrator, Derivative, Transfer Fcn, etc.) are, by definition, continuous.
- Constant blocks (for example, Constant) are, by definition, constant.
- Discrete blocks (e.g., Zero-Order Hold, Unit Delay, Discrete Transfer Fcn, etc.) have sample times that are explicitly specified by the user on the block dialog boxes.
- All other blocks have implicitly defined sample times that are based on the sample times of their inputs. For instance, a Gain block that follows an Integrator is treated as a continuous block, whereas a Gain block that follows a Zero-Order Hold is treated as a discrete block having the same sample time as the Zero-Order Hold block.

  For blocks whose inputs have different sample times, if all sample times are integer multiples of the fastest sample time, the block is assigned the sample time of the fastest input. If a variable-step solver is being used, the block is assigned the continuous sample time. If a fixed-step solver is being used and the greatest common divisor of the sample times (the fundamental sample time) can be computed, it is used. Otherwise continuous is used.

It is important to note that Mux and Demux blocks are simply grouping operators – signals passing through them retain their timing information. For this reason, the lines emanating from a Demux block may have different colors if they are driven by sources having different sample times. In this case, the Mux and Demux blocks are color coded as hybrids (yellow) to indicate that they handle signals with multiple rates.

Similarly, Subsystem blocks that contain blocks with differing sample times are also colored as hybrids, because there is no single rate associated with them. If all of the blocks within a subsystem run at a single rate, then the Subsystem block is colored according to that rate.

Under some circumstances, Simulink also backpropagates sample times to source blocks if it can do so without affecting the output of a simulation. For instance, in the model below, Simulink recognizes that the Signal Generator block is driving a Discrete-Time Integrator block so it assigns the Signal Generator block and the Gain block the same sample time as the Discrete-Time Integrator block.

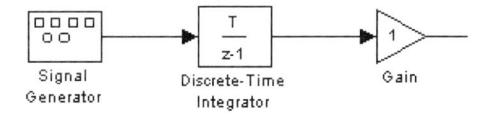

You can verify this by enabling **Sample Time Colors** and noting that all blocks are colored red. Because the Discrete-Time Integrator block only looks at its input at its sample times, this change does not affect the outcome of the simulation but does result in a performance improvement.

Replacing the Discrete-Time Integrator block with a continuous Integrator block, as shown below, and recoloring the model by choosing **Update Diagram** from the **Edit** menu cause the Signal Generator and Gain blocks to change to continuous blocks, as indicated by their being colored black.

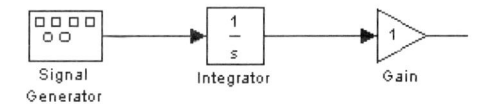

Mixed Continuous and Discrete Systems

Mixed continuous and discrete systems are composed of both sampled and continuous blocks. Such systems can be simulated using any of the integration methods, although certain methods are more efficient and accurate than others. For most mixed continuous and discrete systems, the Runge-Kutta variable step methods, ode23 and ode45, are superior to the other methods in terms of efficiency and accuracy. Due to discontinuities associated with the sample and hold of the discrete blocks, the ode15s and ode113 methods are not recommended for mixed continuous and discrete systems.

7 Additional Topics

Simulink Debugger

Introduction	8-2
Using the Debugger	8-3
Running a Simulation Incrementally	8-6
Setting Breakpoints	8-9
Displaying Information About the Simulation	8-13
Displaying Information About the Model	8-17
Debugger Command Reference	8-21

8 Simulink Debugger

Introduction

The Simulink debugger is a tool for locating and diagnosing bugs in a Simulink model. It enables you to pinpoint problems by running simulations step-by-step and displaying intermediate block states and input and outputs. The following sections describe how to use the debugger to diagnose problems in Simulink models.

Using the Debugger

Starting the Debugger

Use the `sldebug command` or the debug option of the `sim` command to start a model under debugger control. (See `sim` in the online documentation for information on specifying `sim` options.)

For example, either the command

```
sim('vdp',[0,10],simset('debug','on'))
```

or the command

```
sldebug 'vdp'
```

loads the Simulink demo model, vdp, into memory and pauses at the first block in the first time step. The debugger highlights the model's initial block and associated output signal lines in the model diagram. The next figure shows the vdp block diagram as it appears on debug mode start-up.

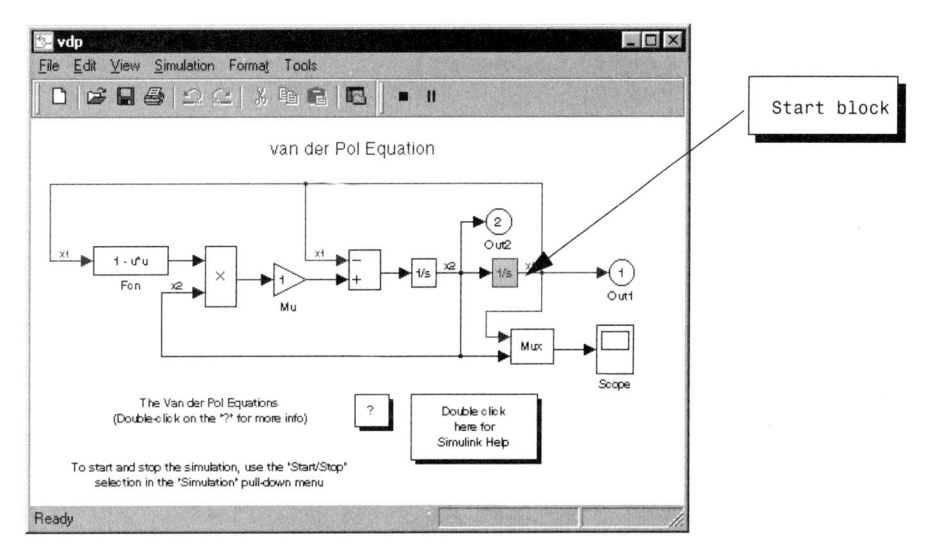

The debugger also prints the simulation start time and a debug command prompt in the MATLAB command window. The command prompt displays the block index (see "About Block Indexes" on page 8-4) and name of the first block to be executed. For example, the command in the preceding example results in the following output in the MATLAB command window.

```
[Tm=0                      ] **Start** of system 'vdp' outputs
(sldebug @0:0 'vdp/Integrator1'): step
```

At this point, you can get help, run the simulation step-by-step, examine data, or perform other debugging tasks by entering debugger and other MATLAB commands at the debug prompt. The following sections explain how to use the debugger commands.

Getting Help

You can get a brief description of the debugger commands by typing help at the debug prompt. For a detailed description of each command, refer to the debugger command reference at the end of this chapter. The following sections show how to use these commands to debug a model.

Entering Commands

The debugger accepts abbreviations for debugger commands. You can also repeat some commands by entering an empty command (i.e., by pressing the **Return** key) at the MATLAB command line. See "Debugger Command Reference" on page 8-21 for a list of command abbreviations and repeatable commands.

About Block Indexes

Many Simulink debugger commands and messages use block indexes to refer to blocks. A block index has the form s:b where s is an integer identifying a system in the model being debugged and b is an integer identifying a block within that system. For example, the block index 0:1 refers to block 1 in the model's 0 system. The slist command shows the block index for each block in the model being debugged (see slist in the online documentation).

Accessing the MATLAB Workspace

You can type any MATLAB expression at the sldebug prompt. For example, suppose you are at a breakpoint and you are logging time and output of your model as tout and yout. Then, the following command

```
(sldebug ...) plot(tout, yout)
```

creates a plot. Suppose you would like to access a variable whose name is the same as the complete or incomplete name of an sldebug command, for example, s, which is a partial completion for the step command. Typing an s at the sldebug prompt steps the model. However,

    (sldebug...) eval('s')

displays the value of the variable s.

Running a Simulation Incrementally

The Simulink debugger lets you run a simulation step by step. You can step from block to block, time point to time point, or from breakpoint to breakpoint (see "Setting Breakpoints" on page 8-9). You select the amount to advance the simulation by entering the appropriate debugger command.

Command	How Simulation Advances
`step`	One block
`next`	One time step
`continue`	To next breakpoint
`run`	To end of simulation, ignoring breakpoints

Stepping by Blocks

To advance a simulation one block, enter `step` at the debugger prompt. The debugger executes the current block, stops, and highlights the next block in the model's block execution order (see "Displaying a Model's Block Execution Order" on page 8-17). For example, the following figure shows the vdp block diagram after execution of the model's first block.

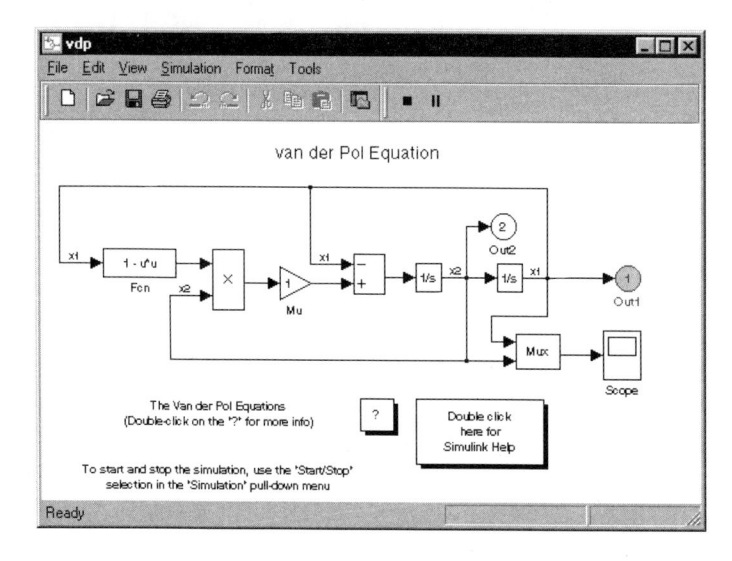

Running a Simulation Incrementally

If the next block to be executed occurs in a subsystem block, the debugger opens the subsystem's block diagram and highlights the next block.

After executing a block, the debugger prints the block's inputs (U) and outputs (Y) and redisplays the debug command prompt in the MATLAB command window. The debugger prompt shows the next block to be evaluated.

```
(sldebug @0:0 'vdp/Integrator1'): step
U1 = [0]
Y1 = [2]
(sldebug @0:1 'vdp/Out1'):
```

Crossing a Time Step Boundary

When you step through the last block in the model's sorted list, the debugger advances the simulation to the next time step and halts the simulation at the beginning of the first block to be executed in the next time step. To signal that you have crossed a time step boundary, the debugger prints the current time in the MATLAB command window. For example, stepping through the last block of the first time step of the vdp model results in the following output in the MATLAB command window.

```
(sldebug @0:8 'vdp/Sum'): step
U1 = [2]
U2 = [0]
Y1 = [-2]
[Tm=0.0001004754572603832  ] **Start** of system 'vdp' outputs
```

Stepping by Minor Time Steps

You can step by blocks within minor time steps, as well as within major steps. To step by blocks within minor time steps, enter minor at the debugger command prompt.

Stepping by Time Steps

The next command executes the remaining blocks in the current time step. In effect, it enables you to advance the simulation to the next time step with a single command. This is convenient when you know that nothing of interest happens in the remainder of the current time step. After advancing the simulation to the next time step, the debugger breaks at the first block in the model's sorted list. For example, entering next after starting the vdp model in debug mode causes the following message to appear in the MATLAB command window.

    [Tm=0.0001004754572603832] **Start** of system 'vdp' outputs

Stepping by Breakpoints

The `continue` command advances the simulation from the current breakpoint to the next breakpoint (see "Setting Breakpoints" on page 8-9) or to the end of the simulation, whichever comes first.

Running a Simulation Nonstop

The `run` command lets you run a program from the current point in the simulation to the end, skipping any intervening breakpoints. At the end of the simulation, the debugger returns you to the MATLAB command line. To continue debugging a model, you must restart the debugger (see "Starting the Debugger" on page 8-3).

Setting Breakpoints

The Simulink debugger allows you to define stopping points in a simulation called breakpoints. You can then run a simulation from breakpoint to breakpoint, using the debugger's `continue` command. The debugger lets you define two types of breakpoints: unconditional and conditional. An unconditional breakpoint occurs whenever a simulation reaches a block or time step that you specified previously. A conditional breakpoint occurs when a condition that you specified in advance arises in the simulation.

Breakpoints come in handy when you know that a problem occurs at a certain point in your program or when a certain condition occurs. By defining an appropriate breakpoint and running the simulation via the `continue` command, you can skip immediately to the point in the simulation where the problem occurs.

You set a particular kind of breakpoint by entering the appropriate breakpoint command.

Command	Where Simulation Stops
`break <gcb	s:b>`	At the beginning of a block
`bafter <gcb	s:b>`	At the end of a block
`tbreak [t]`	At a simulation time step
`nanbreak`	At the occurrence of an underflow or overflow (`NaN`) or infinite (`Inf`) value
`xbreak`	When the simulation reaches the state that determines the simulation step size.
`zcbreak`	When a zero-crossing occurs between simulation time steps.

Breaking at Blocks

The debugger lets you specify a breakpoint at the beginning or end of a block.

Breaking at a Block's Beginning

The break command lets you set a breakpoint at the beginning of a block. Setting a breakpoint at the beginning of a block causes the debugger to stop the simulation when it reaches the block on each time step.

You can specify the block on which to set the breakpoint via a block index or graphically. To specify the block graphically, select the block in the model's block diagram and enter

    break gcb

as shown in the following figure.

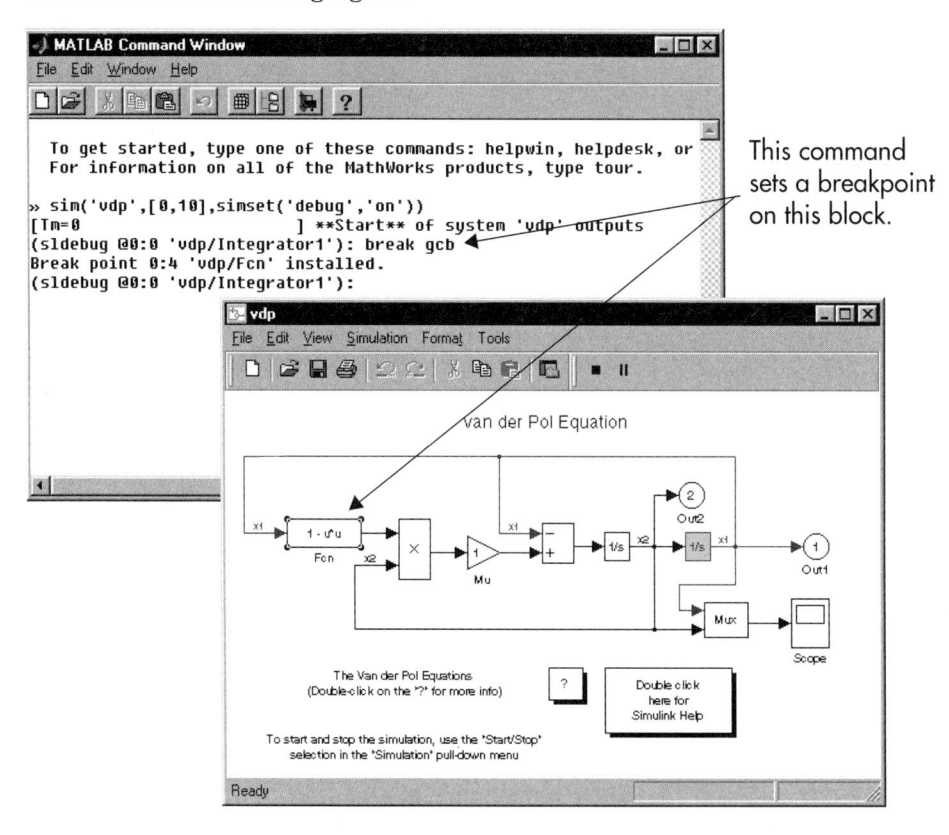

To specify the block via its index, enter

    break s:b

where `s:b` is the block's index (see "About Block Indexes" on page 8-4).

Note You cannot set a breakpoint on a virtual block. A virtual block is a block whose function is purely graphical: it indicates a grouping or relationship among a model's computational blocks. The debugger warns you if you attempt to set a breakpoint on a virtual block. You can obtain a listing of a model's nonvirtual blocks, using the `slist` command (see "Displaying a Model's Nonvirtual Blocks" on page 8-18).

Breaking at a Block's End

The `bafter` command sets a breakpoint at the end of a nonvirtual block. As with `break`, you can specify the block graphically or via its block index.

Clearing Breakpoints from Blocks

The `clear` command clears a breakpoint from the beginning or end of a block. You can specify the block by entering its block index or by selecting the block in the model diagram and entering `gcb` as the argument of the `clear` command.

Breaking at Time Steps

You can use the `tbreak` command to set a breakpoint at a particular time step. The `tbreak` command takes a time value as its only argument. It causes the debugger to stop the simulation at the beginning of the first time step that follows the specified time. For example, starting `vdp` in debug mode and entering the commands

```
tbreak 9
continue
```

causes the debugger to halt the simulation at the beginning of time step `9.0785` as indicated by the output of the `continue` command.

```
[Tm=9.07847133212036        ] **Start** of system 'vdp' outputs
```

Breaking on Nonfinite Values

The `nanbreak` command stops a simulation when the simulation computes a value that is infinite or outside the range of values that can be represented by

8-11

the machine running the simulation. The nanbreak command is useful for pinpointing computational errors in a Simulink model.

Breaking on Step-Size Limiting Steps

The xbreak command causes the debugger to stop the simulation when the model uses a variable-step solver and the solver encounters a state that limits the size of the steps that it can take. This command is useful in debugging models that appear to require an excessive number of simulation time steps to solve.

Breaking at Zero-Crossings

The zcbreak command causes the simulation to halt when Simulink detects a non-sampled zero crossing in a model that includes blocks where zero-crossings can arise. After halting, Simulink prints the location in the model, the time, and the type (rising or falling) of the zero-crossing. For example, setting a zero-crossing break at the start of execution of the zeroxing demo model

```
sldebug zeroxing
[Tm=0                      ] **Start** of system 'zeroxing' outputs
(sldebug @0:0 'zeroxing/Sine Wave'): zcbreak
Break at zero crossing events is enabled.
```

and continuing the simulation

```
(sldebug @0:0 'zeroxing/Sine Wave'): continue
```

results in a rising zero-crossing break at

```
[Tm=0.34350110879329       ] Breaking at block 0:2

[Tm=0.34350110879329       ] Rising zero crossing on 3rd zcsignal
in block 0:2 'zeroxing/Saturation'
```

If a model does not include blocks capable of producing nonsampled zero-crossings, the command prints a message advising you of this fact.

Displaying Information About the Simulation

The Simulink debugger provides a set of commands that allow you to display block states, block inputs and outputs, and other information while running a model.

Displaying Block I/O

The debugger provides three commands for displaying block I/O. Each displays the I/O of a specified block. The main difference among them is when they display the I/O.

Command	When a Block's I/O Is Displayed
probe	Immediately
disp	At every breakpoint
trace	Whenever the block is executed

probe Command

The `probe` command prints the current inputs and outputs of a block that you specify. The command prints the block's I/O in the MATLAB command window.

Command	Description
probe	Enter or exit probe mode. In probe mode, the debugger displays the current inputs and outputs of any block that you select in the model's block diagram. Typing any command causes the debugger to exit probe mode.
probe gcb	Displays I/O of selected block.
probe s:b	Prints the I/O of the block specified by system number s and block number b.

The `probe` command comes in handy when you need to examine the I/O of a block whose I/O is not otherwise displayed. For example, suppose you are using the `step` command to run a model block by block. Each time you step the model, the debugger displays the inputs and outputs of the current block. The `probe` command lets you examine the I/O of other blocks as well. Similarly, suppose you are using the next command to step through a model by time steps. The `next` command does not display block I/O. However, if you need to examine a block's I/O after entering a `next` command, you can do so, using the probe command.

disp Command

The `disp` command causes the debugger to display a specified block's inputs and outputs whenever it halts the simulation. You can specify a block either by entering its block index or by selecting it in the block diagram and entering `gcb` as the `disp` command argument. You can remove any block from the debugger's list of display points, using the `undisp` command. For example, to remove block 0:0, either select the block in the model diagram and enter `undisp gcb` or simply enter `undisp 0:0`.

The `disp` command is useful when you need to monitor the I/O of a specific block or set of blocks as you step through a simulation. Using the `disp` command, you can specify the blocks you want to monitor and the debugger will then redisplay the I/O of those blocks on every step. Note that the debugger always displays the I/O of the current block when you step through a model block by block, using the `step` command. So, you do not need to use the `disp` command if you are interested in watching only the I/O of the current block.

trace Command

The `trace` command causes the debugger to display a specified block's I/O whenever Simulink evaluates the block. It lets you obtain a complete record of a block's I/O without having to stop the simulation. As with the other block I/O display commands, you can specify the block either by entering its block index or by selecting it in the model diagram. You can remove a block from the debugger's list of trace points, using the `untrace` command.

Displaying Algebraic Loop Information

The `atrace` command causes the debugger to display information about a model's algebraic loops (see "Algebraic Loops" on page 7-7) each time they are solved. The command takes a single argument that specifies the amount of information to display.

Command	Information Displayed for Each Algebraic Loop
atrace 0	No information
atrace 1	The loop variable solution, the number of iterations required to solve the loop, and the estimated solution error
atrace 2	Same as level 1
atrace 3	Level 2 plus the Jacobian matrix used to solve loop
atrace 4	Level 3 plus intermediate solutions of the loop variable

Displaying System States

The states debug command lists the current values of the system's states in the MATLAB command window. For example, the following sequence of commands shows the states of the Simulink bouncing ball demo (bounce) after its first and second time steps.

```
sldebug bounce
[Tm=0                    ] **Start** of system 'bounce' outputs
(sldebug @0:0 'bounce/Position'): states
Continuous state vector (value,index,name):
  10                        0 (0:0 'bounce/Position')
  15                        1 (0:5 'bounce/Velocity')
(sldebug @0:0 'bounce/Position'): next
[Tm=0.01                 ] **Start** of system 'bounce' outputs
(sldebug @0:0 'bounce/Position'): states
Continuous state vector (value,index,name):
  10.1495095                0 (0:0 'bounce/Position')
  14.9019                   1 (0:5 'bounce/Velocity')
```

Displaying Integration Information

The ishow command toggles display of integration information. When enabled, this option causes the debugger to print a message each time that it takes a time step or encounters a state that limits the size of a time step. In the first case, the debugger prints the size of the time step, for example,

```
[Tm=9.996264188473381      ] Step of 0.01 was taken by integrator
```

In the second case, the debugger displays the state that currently determines the size of time steps, for example,

```
[Ts=9.676264188473388      ] Integration limited by 1st state of
block 0:0 'bounce/Position'
```

Displaying Information About the Model

In addition to providing information about a simulation, the debugger can provide you with information about the model that underlies the simulation.

Displaying a Model's Block Execution Order

Simulink determines the order in which to execute blocks at the beginning of a simulation run, during model initialization. During simulation, Simulink maintains a list of blocks sorted by execution order. This list is called the sorted list. You can display the sorted list at any time by typing `slist` at the debugger command prompt. The `slist` command lists the model's blocks in execution order. The list includes the block index for each command.

```
---- Sorted list for 'vdp' [12 blocks, 9 nonvirtual blocks,
directFeed=0]
    0:0     'vdp/Integrator1' (Integrator)
    0:1     'vdp/Out1' (Outport)
    0:2     'vdp/Integrator2' (Integrator)
    0:3     'vdp/Out2' (Outport)
    0:4     'vdp/Fcn' (Fcn)
    0:5     'vdp/Product' (Product)
    0:6     'vdp/Mu' (Gain)
    0:7     'vdp/Scope' (Scope)
    0:8     'vdp/Sum' (Sum)
```

Displaying a Block

To determine which block in a model's diagram corresponds to a particular index, type `bshow s:b` at the command prompt, where `s:b` is the block index. The `bshow` command opens the system containing the block (if necessary) and selects the block in the system's window.

Displaying a Model's Nonvirtual Systems

The `systems` command prints a list of the nonvirtual systems in the model being debugged. For example, the Simulink clutch demo (`clutch`) contains the following systems.

```
sldebug clutch
[Tm=0                        ] **Start** of system 'clutch' outputs
(sldebug @0:0 'clutch/Clutch Pedal'): systems
  0    'clutch'
  1    'clutch/Locked'
  2    'clutch/Unlocked'
```

Note The `systems` command does not list subsystems that are purely graphical in nature, that is, subsystems that the model diagram represents as Subsystem blocks but which Simulink solves as part of a parent system. In Simulink models, the root system and triggered or enabled subsystems are true systems. All other subsystems are virtual (that is, graphical) and hence do not appear in the listing produced by the `systems` command.

Displaying a Model's Nonvirtual Blocks

The `slist` command displays a list of the nonvirtual blocks in a model. The listing groups the blocks by system. For example, the following sequence of commands produces a list of the nonvirtual blocks in the Van der Pol (`vdp`) demo model.

Displaying Information About the Model

```
sldebug vdp
[Tm=0                        ] **Start** of system 'vdp' outputs
(sldebug @0:0 'vdp/Integrator1'): slist
---- Sorted list for 'vdp' [12 blocks, 9 nonvirtual blocks,
directFeed=0]
  0:0    'vdp/Integrator1' (Integrator)
  0:1    'vdp/Out1' (Outport)
  0:2    'vdp/Integrator2' (Integrator)
  0:3    'vdp/Out2' (Outport)
  0:4    'vdp/Fcn' (Fcn)
  0:5    'vdp/Product' (Product)
  0:6    'vdp/Mu' (Gain)
  0:7    'vdp/Scope' (Scope)
  0:8    'vdp/Sum' (Sum)
```

Note The slist command does not list blocks that are purely graphical in nature, that is, blocks that indicate relationships or groupings among computational blocks.

Displaying Blocks with Potential Zero-Crossings

The zclist prints a list of blocks in which nonsampled zero-crossings can occur during a simulation. For example, zclist prints the following list for the clutch sample model.

```
(sldebug @0:0 'clutch/Clutch Pedal'): zclist
  2:3    'clutch/Unlocked/Sign' (Signum)
  0:4    'clutch/Lockup Detection/Velocities Match' (HitCross)
  0:10   'clutch/Lockup Detection/Required Friction
            for Lockup/Abs' (Abs)
  0:11   'clutch/Lockup Detection/Required Friction for
            Lockup/ Relational Operator' (RelationalOperator)
  0:18   'clutch/Break Apart Detection/Abs' (Abs)
  0:20   'clutch/Break Apart Detection/Relational Operator'
            (RelationalOperator)
  0:24   'clutch/Unlocked' (SubSystem)
  0:27   'clutch/Locked' (SubSystem)
```

8-19

Displaying Algebraic Loops

The ashow command highlights a specified algebraic loop or the algebraic loop that contains a specified block. To highlight a specified algebraic loop, type ashow s#n, where s is the index of the system (see "Displaying a Model's Block Execution Order" on page 8-17) that contains the loop and n is the index of the loop in the system. To display the loop that contains the currently selected block, enter ashow gcb. To show a loop that contains a specified block, type ashow s:b, where s:b is the block's index. To clear algebraic-loop highlighting from the model diagram, enter ashow clear.

Displaying Debug Settings

The status command displays the settings of various debug options, such as conditional breakpoints. For example, the following sequence of commands displays the initial debug settings for the vdp model.

```
sim('vdp',[0,10],simset('debug','on'))
[Tm=0                    ] **Start** of system 'vdp' outputs
(sldebug @0:0 'vdp/Integrator1'): status
  Current simulation time: 0 (MajorTimeStep)
  Last command: ""
  Stop in minor times steps is disabled.
  Break at zero crossing events is disabled.
  Break when step size is limiting by a state is disabled.
  Break on non-finite (NaN,Inf) values is disabled.
  Display of integration information is disabled.
  Algebraic loop tracing level is at 0.
```

Debugger Command Reference

Table 8-1 lists the debugger commands. The table's Repeat column specifies whether pressing the **Return** key at the command line repeats the command. Detailed descriptions of the commands follow the table.

Table 8-1: Debugger Commands

Command	Short Form	Repeat	Description
ashow	as	No	Show an algebraic loop.
atrace	at	No	Set algebraic loop trace level.
bafter	ba	No	Insert a breakpoint after execution of a block.
break	b	No	Insert a breakpoint before execution of a block.
bshow	bs	No	Show a specified block.
clear	cl	No	Clear a breakpoint from a block.
continue	c	Yes	Continue the simulation.
disp	d	Yes	Display a block's I/O when the simulation stops.
help	? or h	No	Display help for debugger commands.
ishow	i	No	Enable or disable display of integration information.
minor	m	No	Enable or disable minor step mode.
nanbreak	na	No	Set or clear break on nonfinite value.
next	n	Yes	Go to start of the next time step.
probe	p	No	Display a block's I/O.
quit	q	No	Abort simulation.

Table 8-1: Debugger Commands (Continued)

Command	Short Form	Repeat	Description
run	r	No	Run the simulation to completion.
slist	sli	No	List a model's nonvirtual blocks.
states	state	No	Display current state values.
status	stat	No	Display debugging options in effect.
step	s	Yes	Step to next block.
stop	sto	No	Stop the simulation.
systems	sys	No	List a model's nonvirtual systems.
tbreak	tb	No	Set or clear a time breakpoint.
trace	tr	Yes	Display a block's I/O each time it executes.
undisp	und	Yes	Remove a block from the debugger's list of display points.
untrace	unt	Yes	Remove a block from the debugger's list of trace point.
xbreak	x	No	Break when the debugger encounters a step-size-limiting state.
zcbreak	zcb	No	Break at nonsampled zero-crossing events.
zclist	zcl	No	List blocks containing nonsampled zero crossings.

Simulink Quick Reference

Introduction	A-2
Continuous Library Blocks	A-2
Debugger Commands	A-2
Discrete Library Blocks	A-2
Functions & Tables Library Blocks	A-3
Math Library Blocks	A-3
Model Construction Commands	A-3
Nonlinear Library Blocks	A-4
Signals & Systems Library Blocks	A-4
Sinks Library Blocks	A-4
Sources Library Blocks	A-5

A Simulink Quick Reference

Introduction

You can view complete information about any of these blocks from the Help Desk:

1 Select **Using Simulink**.

2 Scroll down to the **Block Reference** section and select the desired block.

Continuous Library Blocks

Memory	Output the block input from the previous time step.
State-Space	Implement a linear state-space system.
Transfer Fcn	Implement a linear transfer function.
Transport Delay	Delay the input by a given amount of time.
Variable Transport Delay	Delay the input by a variable amount of time.
Zero-Pole	Implement a transfer function specified in terms of poles and zeros.

Debugger Commands

ashow	Show an algebraic loop.
atrace	Set algebraic loop trace level.
bafter	Insert a breakpoint after execution of a block.
break	Insert a breakpoint before execution of a block.
bshow	Show a specified block.
clear	Clear a breakpoint from a block.
continue	Continue the simulation.
disp	Display a block's I/O when the simulation stops.
help	Display help for debugger commands.
ishow	Enable or disable display of integration information.

Debugger Commands (Continued)

minor	Enable or disable minor step mode.
nanbreak	Set or clear break on nonfinite value.
next	Go to start of the next time step.
probe	Display a block's I/O.
quit	Abort simulation.
run	Run the simulation to completion.
slist	List a model's nonvirtual blocks.
states	Display current state values.
status	Display debugging options in effect.
step	Step to next block.
stop	Stop the simulation.
systems	List a model's nonvirtual systems.
tbreak	Set or clear a time breakpoint.
trace	Display a block's I/O each time it executes.
undisp	Remove a block from the debugger's list of display points.
untrace	Remove a block from the debugger's list of trace point.
xbreak	Break when the debugger encounters a step-size-limiting state.
zcbreak	Break at nonsampled zero-crossing events.
zclist	List blocks containing nonsampled zero crossings.

Discrete Library Blocks

Discrete Filter	Implement IIR and FIR filters.
Discrete State-Space	Implement a discrete state-space system.
Discrete Transfer Fcn	Implement a discrete transfer function.

Discrete Library Blocks (Continued)

Discrete Zero-Pole	Implement a discrete transfer function specified in terms of poles and zeros.
Discrete-Time Integrator	Perform discrete-time integration of a signal.

Functions & Tables Library Blocks

Fcn	Apply a specified expression to the input.
Look-Up Table	Perform piecewise linear mapping of the input.
Look-Up Table (2-D)	Perform piecewise linear mapping of two inputs.
MATLAB Fcn	Apply a MATLAB function or expression to the input.
S-Function	Access an S-function.

Math Library Blocks

Abs	Output the absolute value of the input.
Algebraic Constraint	Constrain the input signal to zero.
Combinatorial Logic	Implement a truth table.
Complex to Magnitude-Angle	Output the phase and magnitude of a complex input signal.
Complex to Real-Imag	Output the real and imaginary parts of a complex input signal.
Derivative	Output the time derivative of the input.
Dot Product	Generate the dot product.
Gain	Multiply block input.
Logical Operator	Perform the specified logical operation on the input.

Math Library Blocks (Continued)

Magnitude-Angle to Complex	Output a complex signal from magnitude and phase inputs.
Math Function	Perform a mathematical function.
Matrix Gain	Multiply the input by a matrix.
MinMax	Output the minimum or maximum input value.
Product	Generate the product or quotient of block inputs.
Real-Imag to Complex	Output a complex signal from real and imaginary inputs.
Relational Operator	Perform the specified relational operation on the input.
Rounding Function	Perform a rounding function.
Sign	Indicate the sign of the input.
Slider Gain	Vary a scalar gain using a slider.
Sum	Generate the sum of inputs.
Trigonometric Function	Perform a trigonometric function.

Model Construction Commands

add_block	Add a new block to a system.
add_line	Add a line to a system.
bdroot	Get the name of the root-level system.
delete_block	Delete a block from a system.
delete_line	Delete a line from a system.
find_system	Find a system, block, line, or annotation.
gcb	Get the pathname of the current block.
gcbh	Get the handle of the current block.
gcs	Get the pathname of the current system.
get_param	Get a parameter value.
replace_block	Replace a block in a system.

Model Construction Commands (Continued)

set_param	Set parameter values.
simulink	Open the Simulink block library.

Nonlinear Library Blocks

Backlash	Model the behavior of a system with play.
Coulomb & Viscous Friction	Model discontinuity at zero, with linear gain elsewhere.
Dead Zone	Provide a region of zero output.
Manual Switch	Switch between two inputs.
Multiport Switch	Choose between block inputs.
Quantizer	Discretize input at a specified interval.
Rate Limiter	Limit the rate of change of a signal.
Relay	Switch output between two constants.
Saturation	Limit the range of a signal.
Switch	Switch between two inputs.

Signals & Systems Library Blocks

Bus Selector	Output selected input signals.
Configurable Subsystem	Represent any block selected from a specified library.
Data Store Memory	Define a shared data store.
Data Store Read	Read data from a shared data store.
Data Store Write	Write data to a shared data store.
Data Type Conversion	Convert a signal to another data type.
Demux	Separate a vector signal into output signals.
Enable	Add an enabling port to a subsystem.
From	Accept input from a Goto block.

Signals & Systems Library Blocks (Continued)

Goto	Pass block input to From blocks.
Goto Tag Visibility	Define the scope of a Goto block tag.
Ground	Ground an unconnected input port.
Hit Crossing	Detect crossing point.
IC	Set the initial value of a signal.
Inport	Create an input port for a subsystem or an external input.
Merge	Combine several input lines into a scalar line.
Model Info	Display revision control information in a model.
Mux	Combine several input lines into a vector line.
Outport	Create an output port for a subsystem or an external output.
Probe	Output an input signal's width, sample time, and/or signal type.
Subsystem	Represent a system within another system.
Terminator	Terminate an unconnected output port.
Trigger	Add a trigger port to a subsystem.
Width	Output the width of the input vector.

Sinks Library Blocks

Display	Show the value of the input.
Scope	Display signals generated during a simulation.
Stop Simulation	Stop the simulation when the input is nonzero.
To File	Write data to a file.
To Workspace	Write data to a matrix in the workspace.
XY Graph	Display an X-Y plot of signals using a MATLAB figure window.

Sources Library Blocks

Band-Limited White Noise	Introduce white noise into a continuous system.
Chirp Signal	Generate a sine wave with increasing frequency.
Clock	Display and provide the simulation time.
Constant	Generate a constant value.
Digital Clock	Generate simulation time at the specified sampling interval.
Digital Pulse Generator	Generate pulses at regular intervals.
From File	Read data from a file.
From Workspace	Read data from a matrix defined in the workspace.
Pulse Generator	Generate pulses at regular intervals.
Ramp	Generate a constantly increasing or decreasing signal.
Random Number	Generate normally distributed random numbers.
Repeating Sequence	Generate a repeatable arbitrary signal.
Signal Generator	Generate various waveforms.
Sine Wave	Generate a sine wave.
Step	Generate a step function.
Uniform Random Number	Generate uniformly distributed random numbers.

A

Simulink Quick Reference

Index

A

Abs block
   zero crossings 7-6
absolute tolerance 4-13
   simulation accuracy 4-28
accuracy of simulation 4-28
Adams-Bashforth-Moulton PECE solver 4-11
algebraic loops 7-7
   detection 7-2
   simulation speed 4-28
alignment of blocks 3-11
annotations
   changing font 3-34
   creating 3-34
   definition 3-34
   deleting 3-34
   editing 3-34
   manipulating with mouse and keyboard 3-36
   moving 3-34
   using to document models 3-44
Apply button on Mask Editor 6-9
Assignment mask parameter 6-10
attributes format string 3-18
`AttributesFormatString` block parameter
      3-14, 3-17
autoscale icon drawing coordinates 6-25

B

Backlash block
   zero crossings 7-6
backpropagating sample time 7-17
Backspace key 3-14, 3-33, 3-34
bad link 3-22
Band-Limited White Noise block
   simulation speed 4-28

block
   finding specific 1-7
Block data tips 3-9
block descriptions
   creating 6-6
   entering 6-26
block diagrams, printing 3-49
block dialog boxes
   opening 3-13
block icons
   drawing coordinates 6-24
   font 3-16
   icon frame property 6-23
   icon rotation property 6-24
   icon transparency property 6-24
   properties 6-23
   question marks in 6-21, 6-23
   transfer functions on 6-21
block indexes 8-4
block names
   changing location 3-17
   copied blocks 3-11
   editing 3-16
   flipping location 3-17
   font 3-16
   hiding and showing 3-17
   location 3-16
   rules 3-16
   sequence numbers 3-11, 3-12
block parameters
   copying 3-11, 3-12
   displaying beneath a block icon 3-17
   evaluating 7-2
   modifying 4-2
   prompts 6-10
   scalar expansion 3-18, 3-19

I-1

Index

block priorities
    assigning 3-19
block type of masked block 6-26
blocks 3-9-3-20
    alignment 3-11
    callback parameters 3-42
    callback routines 3-40
    connecting 2-10, 3-27
    connections, checking 7-2
    copying 3-25
    copying from block library 3-21
    copying into models 3-10
    copying to other applications 3-12
    deleting 3-14
    disconnecting 3-18
    discrete 7-13
    drop shadows 3-20
    duplicating 3-12
    grouping to create subsystem 3-39
    library 3-21
    moving between windows 3-12
    moving in a model 2-9, 3-12
    orientation 3-15
    reference 3-21, 3-22
    resizing 3-15
    reversing signal flow through 3-46
    signal flow through 3-15
    under mask 6-9
    updating 7-2
    updating from library 3-23
    vectorization 3-18
Bogacki-Shampine formula 4-11, 4-12
books
    MATLAB-related 1-9
Boolean type checking 4-26
bounding box
    grouping blocks for subsystem 3-39

    selecting objects 3-7
branch lines 3-28, 3-46
Break Library Link menu item 3-23
breaking link to library block 3-23
breakpoints
    clearing from blocks 8-11
    setting 8-9
    setting at beginning of a block 8-10
    setting at end of block 8-11
    setting at timesteps 8-11
    setting on nonfinite values 8-11
    setting on step-size limiting steps 8-12
    setting on zero crossings 8-12
Browser 3-53
building models
    exercise 2-6
    tips 3-44

C

callback parameters
    block 3-42
    model 3-41
callback routines 3-40
canceling a command 3-7
changing
    annotations, font 3-34
    block icons, font 3-16
    block names, font 3-16
    block names, location 3-17
    block size 3-15
    sample time during simulation 7-13
    signal labels, font 3-33
check box control type 6-13
Clear menu item 3-14
Clock block
    example 5-3

Index

Close Browser menu item 3-54
Close button on Mask Editor 6-9
Close menu item 2-3
Close Model menu item 3-54
CloseFcn block callback parameter 3-42
CloseFcn model callback parameter 3-41
colors for sample times 7-15
comp.soft-sys.matlab 1-9
connecting blocks 2-10, 3-27
connecting lines to input ports 2-11
consistency checking 4-24
constant sample time 7-11
Continue menu item 4-5
Control System Toolbox
   linearization 5-5
control type 6-12
   check box 6-13
   edit 6-12
   pop-up 6-13
Copy menu item 3-11, 3-12
copy, definition 3-21
CopyFcn block callback parameter 3-42
copying
   block parameters 3-11, 3-12
   blocks 3-10
   library block into a model 3-21
   signal labels 3-33
Create Mask menu item 6-9
Create Subsystem menu item 3-39
creating
   annotations 3-34
   first mask prompt 6-11
   masked block descriptions 6-6
   masked block icons 6-6
   models 3-3
   signal labels 3-33
   subsystems 3-38–3-43

Cut menu item 3-12, 3-14

D

dbstop if error command 6-17
dbstop if warning command 6-17
Dead Zone block
   zero crossings 7-6
debugger
   getting command help 8-4
   starting 8-3
debugging initialization commands 6-17
decimation factor
   saving simulation output 4-21
default
   solvers 4-10
defining
   mask type 6-6, 6-26
   masked block descriptions 6-26
   masked block help text 6-6
Delete key 3-14, 3-33, 3-34
DeleteFcn block callback parameter 3-42
deleting
   annotations 3-34
   blocks 3-14
   mask prompts 6-12
   signal labels 3-33
demo model, running 2-2
demos
   Simulink 1-6
Derivative block
   linearization 5-5
derivatives
   calculating 7-3
description of masked blocks 6-26
Diagnostics page of Simulation Parameter dialog
   box 4-24

I-3

Index

diagonal line segments 3-28
diagonal lines 3-27
direct feedthrough 7-2
disabling zero crossing detection 4-25, 7-5
disconnecting blocks 3-18
discontinuities
    zero crossings 7-3
discrete blocks 7-13
`discrete` solver 4-10, 4-11, 4-12
Discrete-Time Integrator block
    sample time colors 7-17
discrete-time systems 7-13
`disp` command 6-18
Display Alphabetical List menu item 3-54
Display Hierarchical List menu item 3-54
displaying
    line widths 3-31
    output trajectories 5-2
    transfer functions on masked block icons 6-21
`dlinmod` function 5-4
documentation page of Mask Editor 6-9
Dormand-Prince
    formula 4-12
    pair 4-11
`dpoly` command 6-22
drawing coordinates 6-24
    autoscale 6-25
    normalized 6-7, 6-25
    pixel 6-25
`droots` command 6-23
drop shadows 3-20
duplicating blocks 3-12

E

edit control type 6-12
editing

annotations 3-34
block names 3-16
mask prompts 6-11
models 3-3
signal labels 3-33
Elementary Math block
    algebraic loops 7-7
ending Simulink session 3-57
equations, modeling 3-45
equilibrium point determination 5-7
error tolerance 4-13
    simulation accuracy 4-28
    simulation speed 4-27
Euler's method 4-12
`eval` command and masked block help 6-27
Evaluate Assignment type 6-10
examples
    Clock block 5-3
    continuous system 3-46
    converting Celsius to Fahrenheit 3-45
    equilibrium point determination 5-7
    linearization 5-4
    masking 6-3
    multirate discrete model 7-14
    return variables 5-2
    Scope block 5-2
    To Workspace block 5-3
    Transfer Function block 3-47
Exit MATLAB menu item 2-13, 3-57
Expand All menu item 3-54
Expand Library Links menu item 3-54
extracting linear models 5-4

F

Fcn block
    simulation speed 4-27

Index

file, writing to 4-5
final states, saving 4-21
finding library block 3-24
fixed icon rotation 6-24
fixed step size 4-13
fixed-step solvers 4-9, 4-12
Flip Block menu item 3-15, 3-46
Flip Name menu item 3-17
floating Display block 4-2
floating Scope block 4-2
font
    annotations 3-34
    block icons 3-16
    block names 3-16
    signal labels 3-33
Font menu item 3-16, 3-33
`fprintf` command 6-19
fundamental sample time 4-10

G

Gain block
    and algebraic loops 7-7
Go To Library Link menu item 3-24
grouping blocks 3-38

H

handles on selected object 3-7
help
    sources of 1-8
    via MathWorks Knowledge Base 1-10
    via MathWorks Web site 1-9
    via newsgroup 1-9
Help button on Mask Editor 6-9
Help Desk
    accessing 1-8

help text for masked blocks 6-6, 6-27
Heun's method 4-12
Hide Name menu item 3-17, 3-40
Hide Port Labels menu item 3-40
hiding block names 3-17
hierarchy of model 3-44, 7-2
Hit Crossing block
    zero crossing detection 4-25
    zero crossings 7-4, 7-6
hybrid systems
    integrating 7-17
    simulating 7-13

I

icon frame mask property 6-23
icon page of Mask Editor 6-9
icon rotation mask property 6-24
icon transparency mask property 6-24
icons
    creating for masked blocks 6-6, 6-18
    displaying graphics on 6-20
    displaying images on 6-21
    displaying text on 6-18
    transfer functions on 6-21
improved Euler formula 4-12
`inf` values in mask plotting commands 6-21
`InitFcn` block callback parameter 3-42
`InitFcn` model callback parameter 3-41
initial conditions
    determining 4-22
    specifying 4-21
initial step size 4-12, 4-13
    simulation accuracy 4-28
initialization commands 6-15
    debugging 6-17
initialization page of Mask Editor 6-9

I-5

Inport block
    in subsystem 3-38, 3-39
    linearization 5-4
    supplying input to model 4-17
inputs
    loading from base workspace 4-17
    mixing vector and scalar 3-18
    scalar expansion 3-18
    vector or scalar 3-18
inserting mask prompts 6-11
Integrator block
    algebraic loops 7-7
    example 3-46
    sample time colors 7-17
    simulation speed 4-28
    zero crossings 7-6
invariant constants 7-11
invisible icon frame 6-23

J
Jacobian matrices 4-12

K
keyboard actions, summary 3-35
keyboard command 6-17

L
labeling signals 3-32
labeling subsystem ports 3-40
learning Simulink 1-6
libinfo command 3-24
libraries 3-21-3-26
    searching 3-25
library block

definition 3-21
finding 3-24
library blocks, getting information about 3-24
Library Browser 3-24
library, definition 3-21
limit rows to last check box 4-21
line segments 3-28
    creating 3-29
    diagonal 3-28
    moving 3-29
line vertices, moving 3-30
Line Widths menu item 3-31
linear models, extracting 5-4
linearization 5-4
lines 3-27-3-32
    branch 3-28, 3-46
    carrying the same signal 2-11
    connecting to input ports 2-11
    diagonal 3-27
    dividing into segments 3-29
    manipulating with mouse and keyboard 3-35
    signals carried on 4-2
    widths, displaying 3-31
link
    breaking 3-23
    definition 3-21
    to library block 3-22
    unresolved 3-22
LinkStatus block parameter 3-22
linmod function 5-4
Literal Assignment type 6-10
load initial check box 4-22
LoadFcn block callback parameter 3-42
loading from base workspace 4-17
loading initial states 4-22
location of block names 3-16, 3-17
Look Into System menu item 3-54

Look Under Mask Dialog menu item 3-54
Look Under Mask menu item 6-9
loops, algebraic 7-7

M

manual, organization 1-12
Mask Editor 6-9
mask help text 6-6
Mask Subsystem menu item 6-4, 6-9
mask type 6-6, 6-26
mask workspace 6-5, 6-15
masked blocks
    block descriptions 6-6
    control types 6-12
    description 6-26
    documentation 6-26
    help text 6-27
    icons
        creating 6-6, 6-18
        displaying a transfer function on 6-22
        displaying graphics on 6-20
        displaying images on 6-21
        displaying text on 6-18
        setting properties of 6-23
    initialization commands 6-15
    looking under 6-9
    parameters 6-3
        assigning values to 6-10
        default values 6-14
        prompts for 6-10
        tunable 6-14
        undefined 6-23
    ports
        displaying labels of 6-20
    question marks in icon 6-21, 6-23
    type 6-26

unmasking 6-9
MathWorks Knowledge Base 1-10
MathWorks Store
    purchasing products from 1-9
MathWorks Web site 1-9
MATLAB
    books 1-9
MATLAB Fcn block
    simulation speed 4-27
maximum order of ode15s solver 4-14
maximum step size 4-12, 4-13
maximum step size parameter 4-13
mdl file 3-48
Memory block
    simulation speed 4-27
memory issues 3-44
menus 3-3
MEX-file models, simulating 4-3
M-file models, simulating 4-3
M-file S-functions
    simulation speed 4-27
M-files, running simulation from 4-3
MinMax block
    zero crossings 7-6
mixed continuous and discrete systems 7-17
Model Browser 3-53
model files 3-48
    names 3-48
ModelCloseFcn block callback parameter 3-42
modeling
    equations 3-45
    strategies 3-44
models
    building 2-6
    callback parameters 3-41
    callback routines 3-40
    creating 3-3

editing 3-3
organizing and documenting 3-44
printing 3-49
saving 2-13, 3-48
selecting entire 3-8
tips for building 3-44
mouse actions, summary 3-35
MoveFcn block callback parameter 3-42
moving
annotations 3-34
blocks and lines 3-12
blocks between windows 3-12
blocks in a model 2-9, 3-12
line segments 3-29
line vertices 3-30
mask prompts 6-12
signal labels 3-33
multirate systems 7-13, 7-14
Mux block
changing number of input ports 2-10

N

NameChangeFcn block callback parameter 3-42
names
blocks 3-16
copied blocks 3-11
model files 3-48
NaN values in mask plotting commands 6-21
New Library menu item 3-21
New menu item 3-3
newsgroup 1-9
normalized icon drawing coordinates 6-7, 6-25
numerical differentiation formula 4-11
numerical integration 7-3

O

objects
selecting more than one 3-7
selecting one 3-7
ode1 solver 4-12
ode113 solver 4-11
hybrid systems 7-17
Memory block 4-27
ode15s solver 4-10, 4-11, 4-27
hybrid systems 7-17
maximum order 4-14
Memory block 4-27
unstable simulation results 4-28
ode2 solver 4-12
ode23 solver 4-11
hybrid systems 7-17
ode23s solver 4-11, 4-14, 4-28
ode3 solver 4-12
ode4 solver 4-12
ode45 solver 4-10, 4-11
hybrid systems 7-17
ode5 solver 4-12
offset to sample time 7-13
opaque icon 6-24
Open menu item 3-3
Open System menu item 3-54
OpenFcn block callback parameter 3-43, 3-55
OpenFcn model callback parameter 3-56
opening
block dialog boxes 3-13
Subsystem block 3-39
ordering of states 4-22
organization of manual 1-12
orientation of blocks 3-15
Outport block
example 5-2
in subsystem 3-38, 3-39

Index

linearization 5-4
output
   additional 4-16
   options 4-15
   saving to workspace 4-20
   smoother 4-16
   specifying for simulation 4-16
   trajectories, viewing 5-2
   vector or scalar 3-18
   writing to file 4-5
   writing to workspace 4-5, 4-20

P

`PaperOrientation` model parameter 3-51
`PaperPosition` model parameter 3-51
`PaperPositionMode` model parameter 3-51
`PaperType` model parameter 3-51
Parameters menu item 2-12, 4-4, 4-8
`ParentCloseFcn` block callback parameter 3-43
Paste menu item 3-11, 3-12
patches
   acquiring 1-5
Pause menu item 4-5
pixel icon drawing coordinates 6-25
`plot` command and masked block icon 6-20
pop-up control type 6-13
port labels
   displaying 6-20
ports
   block orientation 3-15
   labeling in subsystem 3-40
`PostLoadFcn` model callback parameter 3-41
`PostSaveFcn` block callback parameter 3-43
`PostSaveFcn` model callback parameter 3-41
PostScript file, printing to 3-51
`PreLoadFcn` model callback parameter 3-41

`PreSaveFcn` block callback parameter 3-43
`PreSaveFcn` model callback parameter 3-41
Print (Browser) menu item 3-54
`print` command 3-49
Print menu item 3-49
printing
   block diagrams 3-49
   to PostScript file 3-51
`Priority` block parameter 3-19
proceeding with suspended simulation 4-5
produce additional output option 4-16
produce specified output only option 4-16
product
   registration 1-10
Product block
   algebraic loops 7-7
professional version
   differences with Student Version 1-3
prompts
   control types 6-12
   creating 6-11
   deleting 6-12
   editing 6-11
   inserting 6-11
   masked block parameters 6-10
   moving 6-12
purely discrete systems 7-13

Q

question marks in masked block icon 6-21, 6-23
Quit MATLAB menu item 2-13, 3-57

R

Random Number block
   simulation speed 4-28

Index

Redo menu item 3-5
reference block 3-22
    definition 3-21
reference information, obtaining 1-7
refine factor 4-16
registering your software 1-10
Relational Operator block
    zero crossings 7-6
relative tolerance 4-13
    simulation accuracy 4-28
Relay block
    zero crossings 7-6
resizing blocks 3-15
return variables, example 5-2
reversing direction of signal flow 3-46
Revert button on Mask Editor 6-9
Rosenbrock formula 4-11
Rotate Block menu item 3-15
rotates icon rotation 6-24
Runge-Kutta (2,3) pair 4-11
Runge-Kutta (4,5) formula 4-11
Runge-Kutta fourth-order formula 4-12
running the simulation 2-12

S

sample model 2-6
sample time 7-13
    backpropagating 7-17
    changing during simulation 7-13
    colors 7-15
    constant 7-11
    fundamental 4-10
    offset 7-13
    parameter 7-13
    simulation speed 4-27
Sample Time Colors menu item 7-12, 7-16

sampled data systems 7-13
Saturation block
    zero crossings 7-4, 7-6
Save As menu item 3-48
Save menu item 2-13, 3-48
save options area 4-20
save to workspace area 4-20
save_system command 3-23
saving
    final states 4-21, 4-22
    models 2-13, 3-48
    output to workspace 4-20
scalar expansion 3-18
Scope block
    example 3-47, 5-2
Select All menu item 3-8
selecting
    model 3-8
    more than one object 3-7
    one object 3-7
sequence numbers on block names 3-11, 3-12
Set Font dialog box 3-16
set_param command 3-23
setting breakpoints 8-9
Shampine, L. F. 4-12
Show Browser menu item 3-54
Show Name menu item 3-17
showing block names 3-17
Sign block
    zero crossings 7-6
signal flow through blocks 3-15
signal labels
    changing font 3-33
    copying 3-33
    creating 3-33
    deleting 3-33
    editing 3-33

Index

moving 3-33
    using to document models 3-44
signals 3-27
    labeling 3-32
    vector 3-18
simulation
    accuracy 4-28
    displaying information about
        algebraic loops 8-13, 8-14, 8-20
        block execution order 8-17
        block I/O 8-13
        debug settings 8-20
        integration 8-15
        nonvirtual blocks 8-18
        nonvirtual systems 8-18
        system states 8-15
        zero crossings 8-19
    menu 4-4
    proceeding with suspended 4-5
    running 2-12
    running incrementally 8-6
    speed 4-27
    starting 4-4
    stepping by blocks 8-6
    stepping by breakpoints 8-8
    stepping by time steps 8-7
    stopping 2-13, 4-5
    suspending 4-5
Simulation Diagnostics dialog box 4-6
simulation parameters 4-8
    setting 4-4
    specifying 2-12, 4-4
Simulation Parameters dialog box 2-12, 4-4, 4-8-4-25
simulation time
    compared to clock time 4-9
    writing to workspace 4-20

Simulink
    demos 1-6
    ending session 3-57
    how to learn 1-6
    icon 3-2
    menus 3-3
    starting 3-2
    windows and screen resolution 3-5
Simulink block library 3-2
`simulink` command 3-2
size of block, changing 3-15
sizes vector 4-22
`sldebug` command 8-3
Solution Search Engine 1-10
Solver page of Simulation Parameters dialog box 4-8
solvers 4-9-4-12
    changing during simulation 4-2
    choosing 4-4
    default 4-10
    `discrete` 4-10, 4-11, 4-12
    fixed-step 4-9, 4-12
    `ode1` 4-12
    `ode113` 4-11, 4-27
    `ode15s` 4-10, 4-11, 4-14, 4-27, 4-28
    `ode2` 4-12
    `ode23` 4-11
    `ode23s` 4-11, 4-14, 4-28
    `ode3` 4-12
    `ode4` 4-12
    `ode45` 4-10, 4-11
    `ode5` 4-12
    variable-step 4-9, 4-11
speed of simulation 4-27
`stairs` function 7-14
Start menu item 2-2, 2-12, 3-46, 4-4
start time 4-9

I-11

Index

StartFcn block callback parameter 3-43
StartFcn model callback parameter 3-41
starting Simulink 3-2
state events 7-3
states
    determining 7-3
    initial 4-22
    loading initial 4-22
    ordering of 4-22
    saving final 4-21, 4-22
    updating 7-13
    writing to workspace 4-20
State-Space block
    algebraic loops 7-7
status bar 3-5
Step block
    zero crossings 7-6
step size 4-12
    simulation speed 4-27
stiff problems 4-12
stiff systems and simulation time 4-27
Stop menu item 2-3, 2-13, 4-5
stop time 4-9
Stop Time parameter 2-13
StopFcn block callback parameter 3-43
StopFcn model callback parameter 3-41
Student Version
    differences with professional version 1-3
    MATLAB differences 1-3
    Simulink differences 1-4
Subsystem block
    adding to create subsystem 3-38
    opening 3-39
    zero crossings 7-7
subsystems
    creating 3-38-3-43
    labeling ports 3-40

    model hierarchy 3-44
    underlying blocks 3-39
Sum block
    algebraic loops 7-7
summary of mouse and keyboard actions 3-35
support
    sources of 1-8
suspending simulation 4-5
Switch block
    zero crossings 7-7

T

technical support 1-10
terminating MATLAB 2-13
terminating Simulink 2-13
terminating Simulink session 3-57
text command 6-18
time interval and simulation speed 4-27
tips for building models 3-44
To Workspace block
    example 5-3
Transfer Fcn block
    algebraic loops 7-7
    example 3-47
    linearization 5-5
transfer functions
    masked block icons 6-21
transparent icon 6-24
Transport Delay block
    linearization 5-5
trim function 5-7
troubleshooting 1-8
tunable parameters 6-14

Index

U
Undo menu item 3-7
UndoDeleteFcn block callback parameter 3-43
Unmask button on Mask Editor 6-9
unresolved link 3-22
unstable simulation results 4-28
Update Diagram menu item 3-18, 3-22, 3-23, 7-16
updates
    acquiring 1-5
updating linked blocks 3-23
updating states 7-13
URL specification in block help 6-27

V
variable-step solvers 4-9, 4-11
vdp model
    initial conditions 4-23
vector length, checking 7-2
vectorization of blocks 3-18
vertices, moving 3-30
viewing output trajectories 5-2
virtual blocks 3-9
visible icon frame 6-23

W
web command and masked block help 6-27
Web site 1-9
Wide Vector Lines menu item 3-18
workspace
    loading from 4-17
    mask 6-5, 6-15
    saving to 4-20
    writing to 4-5

Workspace I/O page of Simulation Parameters
    dialog box 4-17
www.mathworks.com 1-9
www.mathworks.com/books 1-9
www.mathworks.com/education 1-9
www.mathworks.com/store 1-9
www.mathworks.com/support 1-8, 1-10

Z
zero crossings 7-3-7-7
    disabling detection of 4-25
Zero-Pole block
    algebraic loops 7-7
Zooming block diagrams 3-6

Index